GRAPHIC LIBRARY

GRAPHIC HISTORY

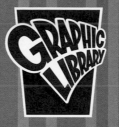

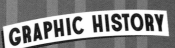

THE ASSASSINATION OF ABRAHAM LINCOLN

by Kay Melchisedech Olson
illustrated by
Otha Zackariah Edward Lohse

Consultant:
Thomas F. Schwartz, PhD
Illinois State Historian
Illinois Historic Preservation Agency
Springfield, Illinois

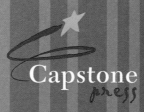

Capstone press
Mankato, Minnesota

Graphic Library is published by Capstone Press,
151 Good Counsel Drive, P.O. Box 669, Mankato, Minnesota 56002.
www.capstonepress.com

Printed in the United States of America

1 2 3 4 5 6 10 09 08 07 06 05

Library of Congress Cataloging-in-Publication Data
Olson, Kay Melchisedech.
The assassination of Abraham Lincoln / by Kay Melchisedech Olson; illustrated by Otha Zackariah Edward Lohse.
p. cm.—(Graphic library. Graphic history)
Includes bibliographical references (p.31) and index.
Audience: Grades 4–6.
ISBN 0-7368-3831-7 (hardcover)
ISBN 0-7368-5241-7 (paperback)
1. Lincoln, Abraham, 1809–1865—Assassination—Juvenile literature. 2. Booth, John Wilkes, 1838–1865—Juvenile literature. I. Lohse, Otha Zackariah Edward. II. Title. III. Series.
E457.5.O48 2005
973.7'092—dc22 2004020300

Summary: In graphic-novel format, tells the story of Abraham Lincoln's assassination and the escape and death of John Wilkes Booth.

Editor's note: Direct quotations from primary sources are indicated by a yellow background.

Direct quotations appear on the following pages:
Page 5 (Lincoln), from *Twenty Days* by Dorothy Meserve Kunhardt and Philip B. Kunhardt Jr. (New York: Castle Books, 1965).
Pages 5 (actor), 8, 19, 21, 27, from *Blood on the Moon* by Edward Steers (Lexington: University Press of Kentucky, 2001).
Pages 13, 20, from *The Day Lincoln Was Shot* by Jim Bishop (New York: Harper & Row, 1955).

Credits
Art Director and Storyboard Artist
Jason Knudson

Art Director
Heather Kindseth

Editor
Tom Adamson

Acknowledgement
Capstone Press thanks Philip Charles Crawford, Library Director, Essex High School, Essex, Vermont, and columnist for *Knowledge Quest*, for his assistance in the preparation of this book.

Table of Contents

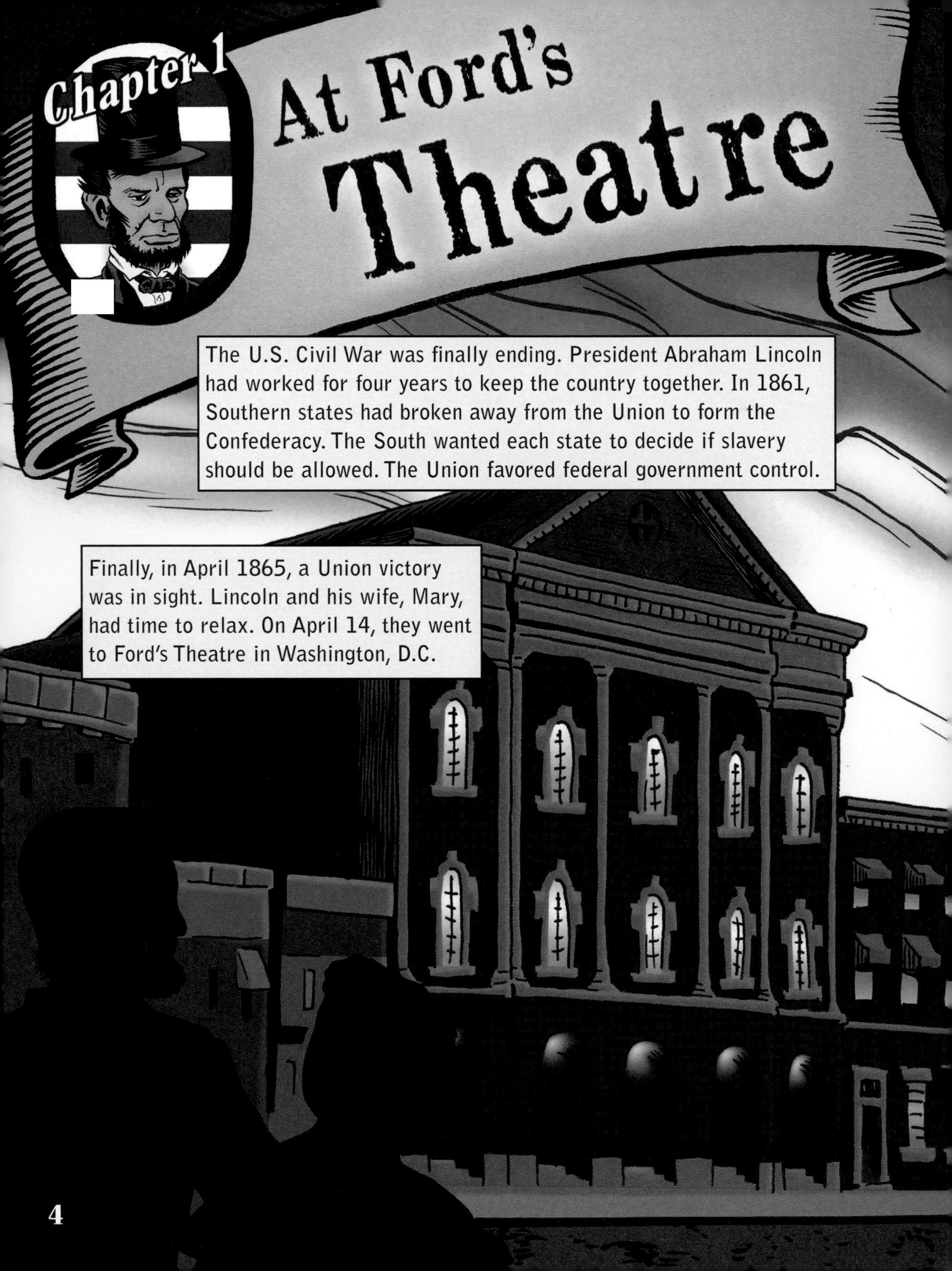
Chapter 1
At Ford's Theatre
The U.S. Civil War was finally ending. President Abraham Lincoln had worked for four years to keep the country together. In 1861, Southern states had broken away from the Union to form the Confederacy. The South wanted each state to decide if slavery should be allowed. The Union favored federal government control.
Finally, in April 1865, a Union victory was in sight. Lincoln and his wife, Mary, had time to relax. On April 14, they went to Ford's Theatre in Washington, D.C.

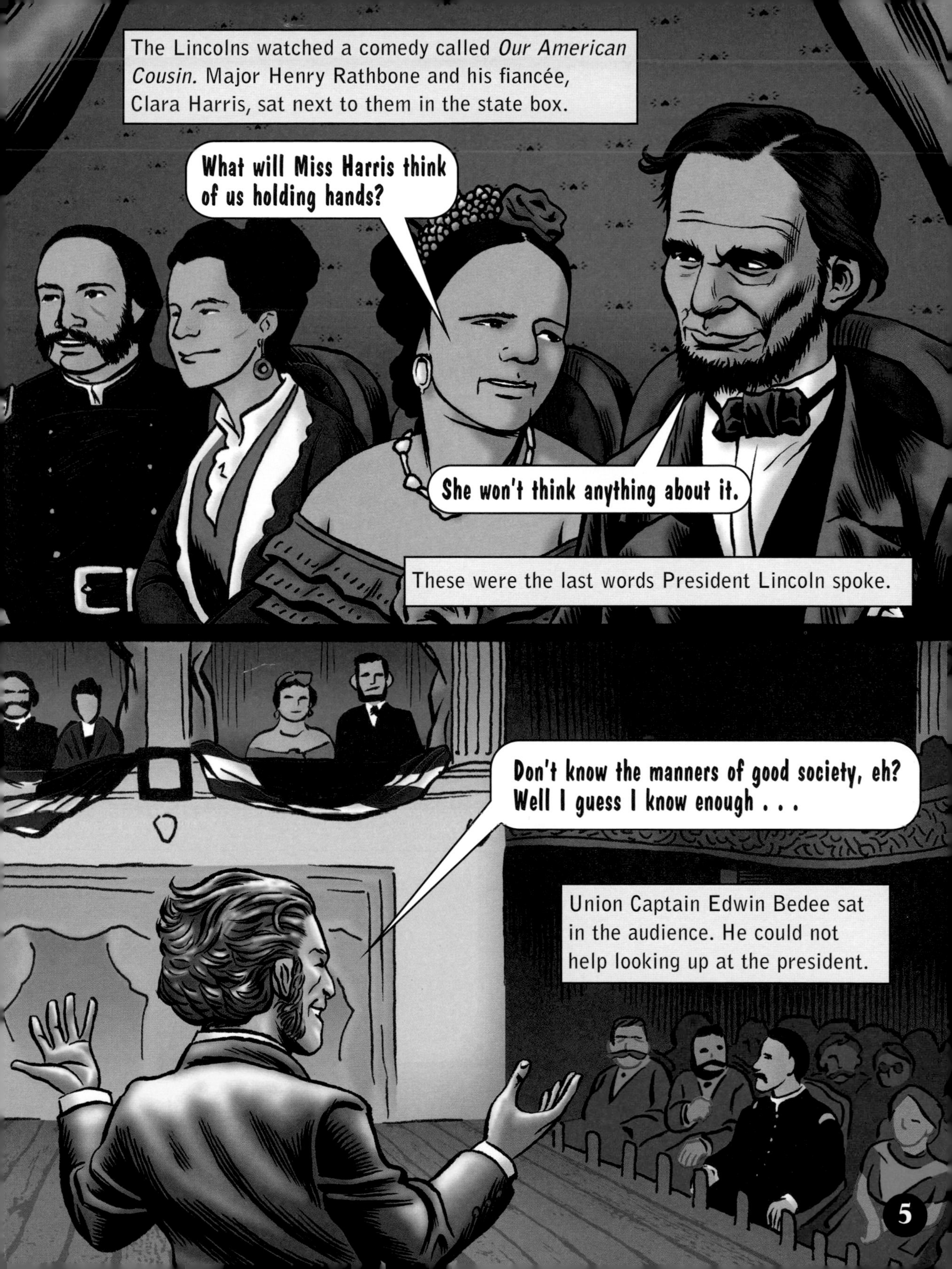
The Lincolns watched a comedy called *Our American Cousin.* Major Henry Rathbone and his fiancée, Clara Harris, sat next to them in the state box.
What will Miss Harris think of us holding hands?
She won't think anything about it.
These were the last words President Lincoln spoke.
Don't know the manners of good society, eh? Well I guess I know enough . . .
Union Captain Edwin Bedee sat in the audience. He could not help looking up at the president.

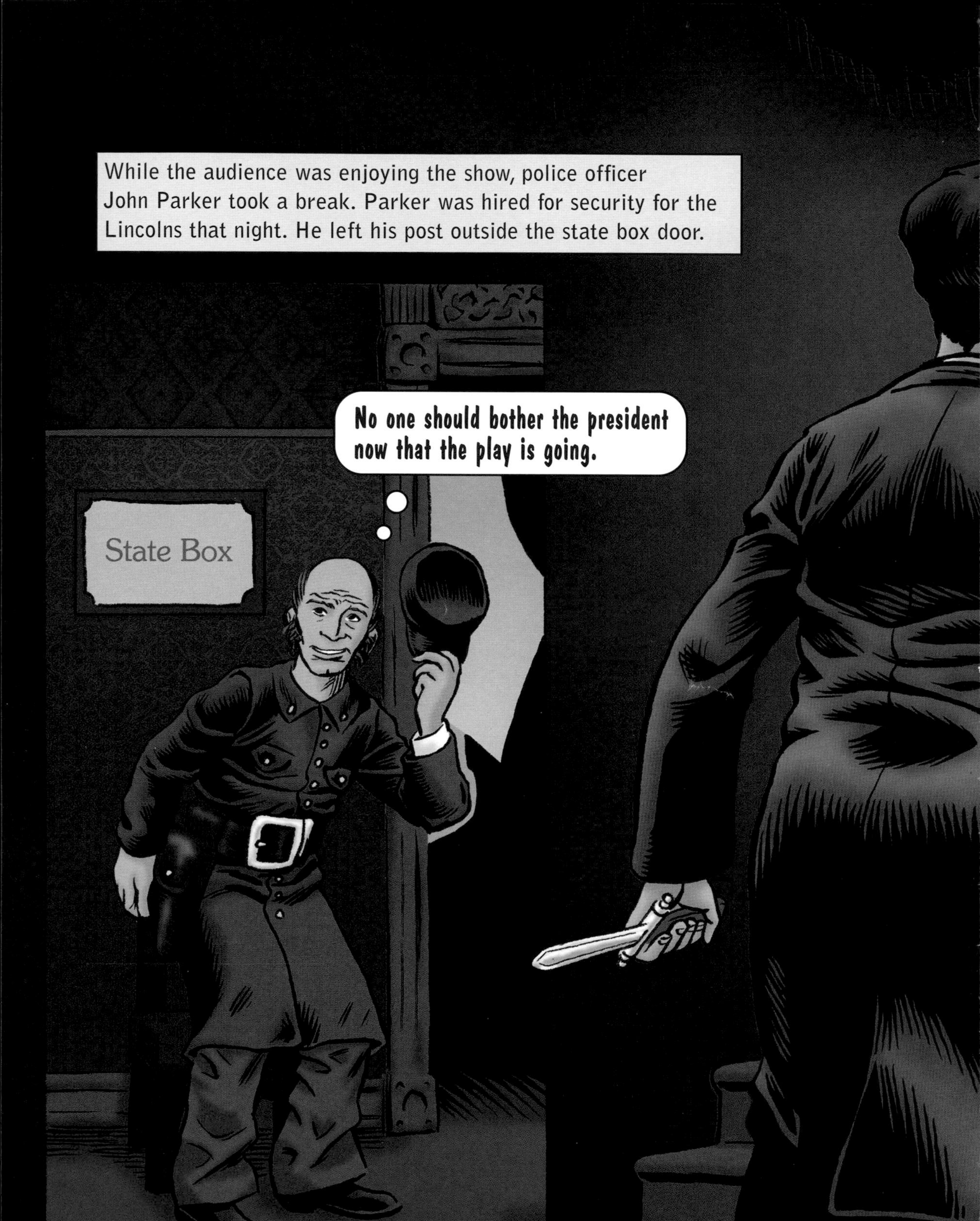
While the audience was enjoying the show, police officer John Parker took a break. Parker was hired for security for the Lincolns that night. He left his post outside the state box door.
State Box
No one should bother the president now that the play is going.

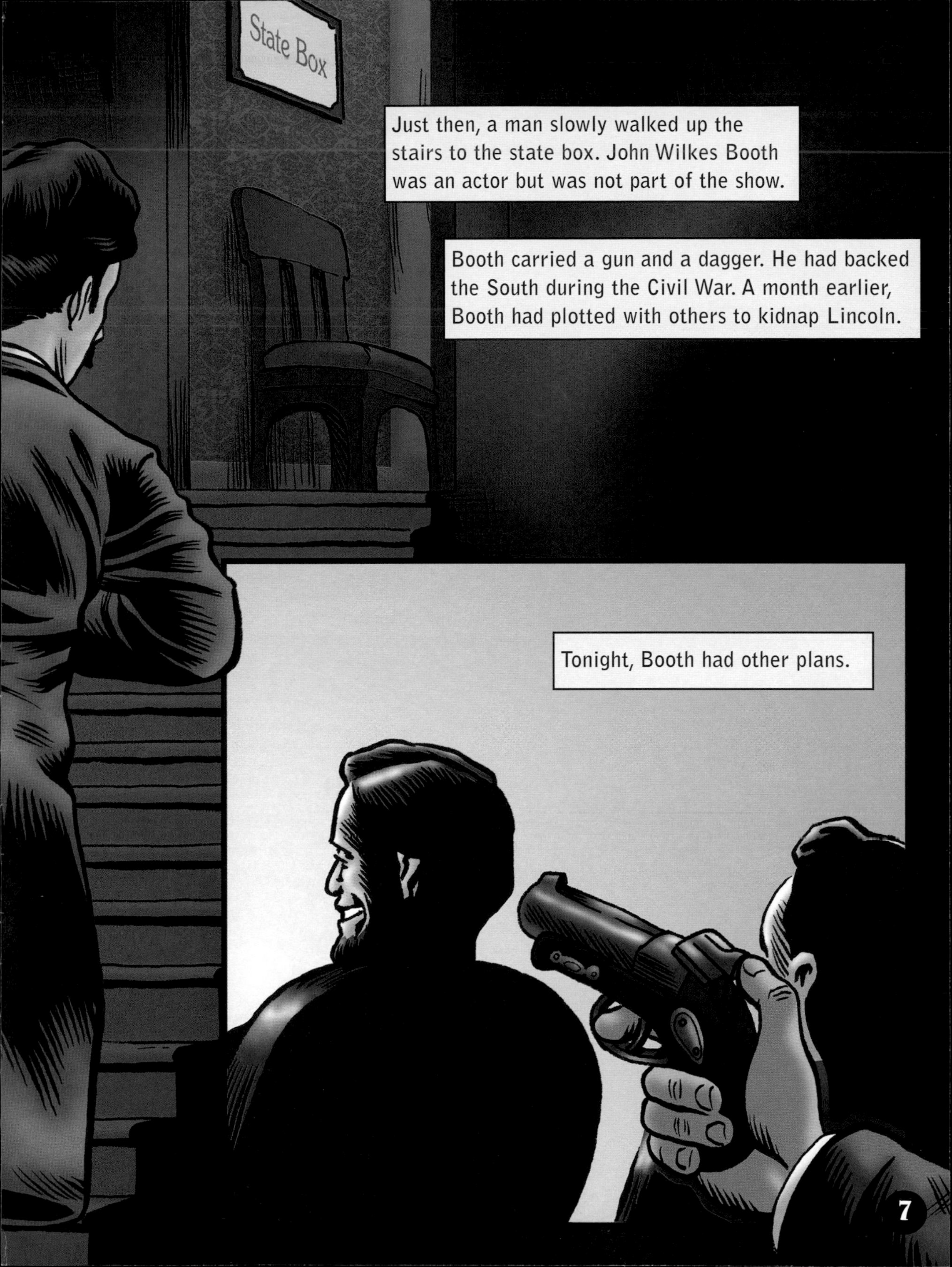
State Box
Just then, a man slowly walked up the stairs to the state box. John Wilkes Booth was an actor but was not part of the show.
Booth carried a gun and a dagger. He had backed the South during the Civil War. A month earlier, Booth had plotted with others to kidnap Lincoln.
Tonight, Booth had other plans.

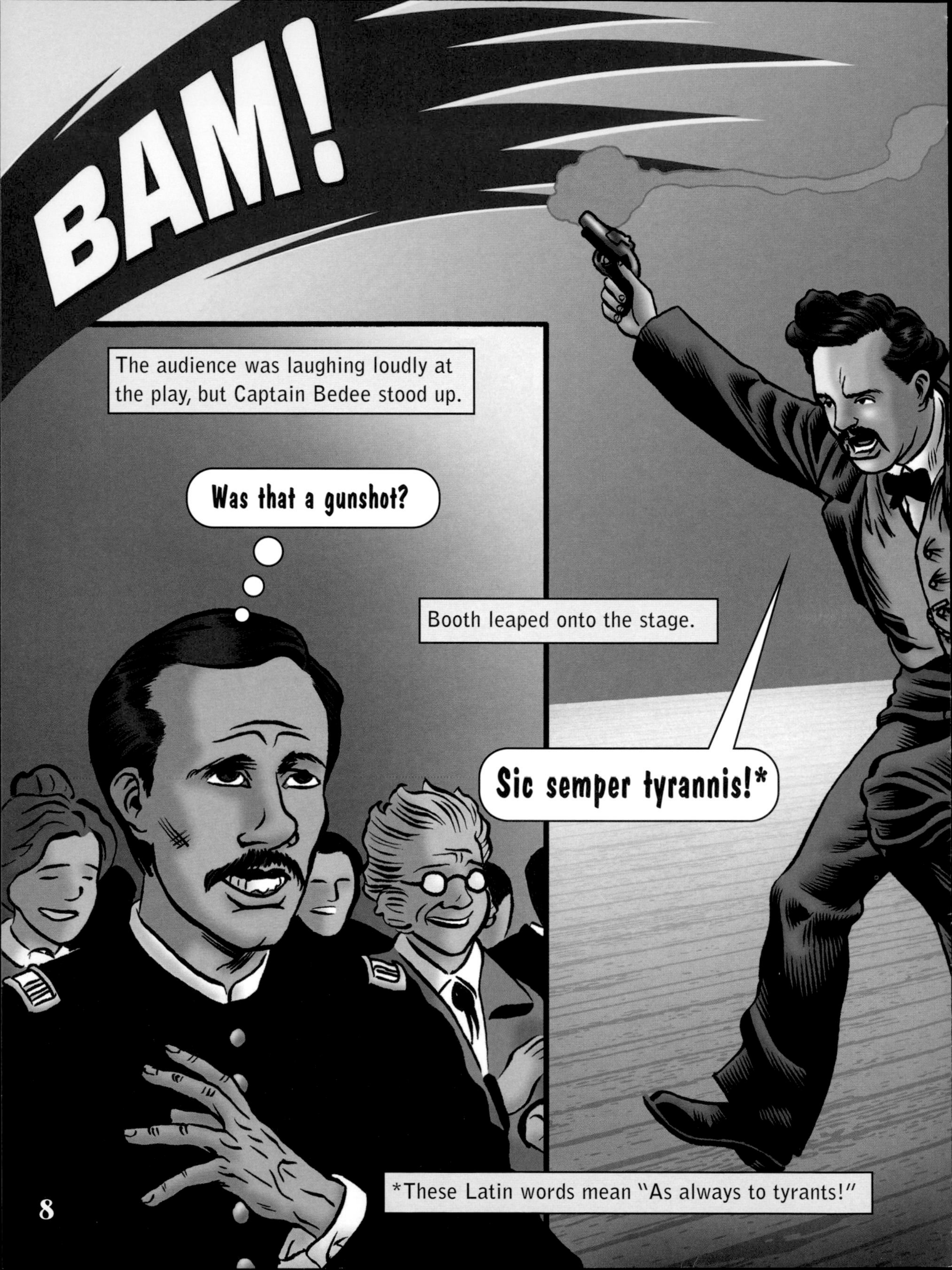
BAM!
The audience was laughing loudly at the play, but Captain Bedee stood up.
Was that a gunshot?
Booth leaped onto the stage.
Sic semper tyrannis!*
*These Latin words mean "As always to tyrants!"

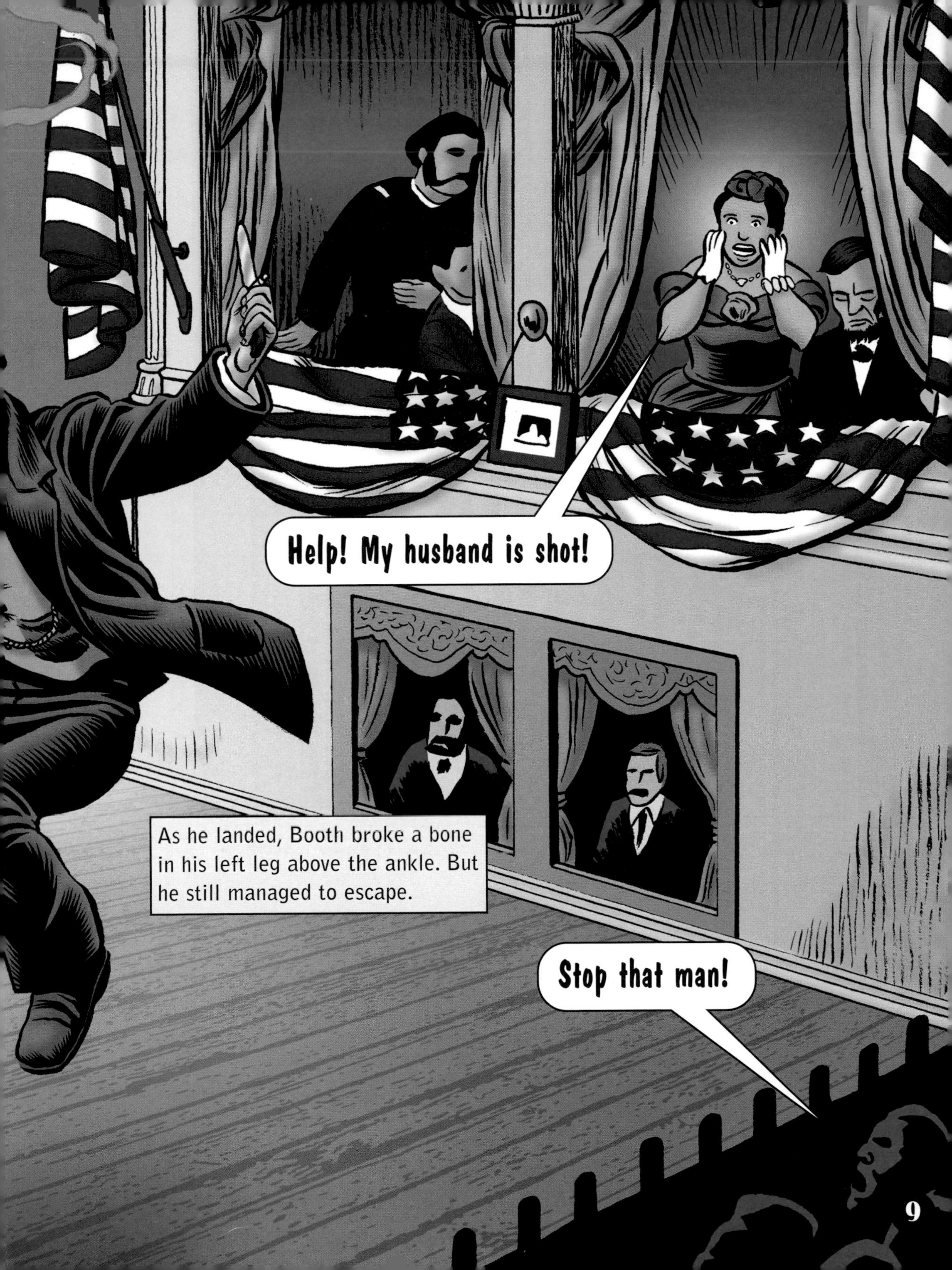
Help! My husband is shot!
As he landed, Booth broke a bone in his left leg above the ankle. But he still managed to escape.
Stop that man!

Chapter 2 Trying to Save the President

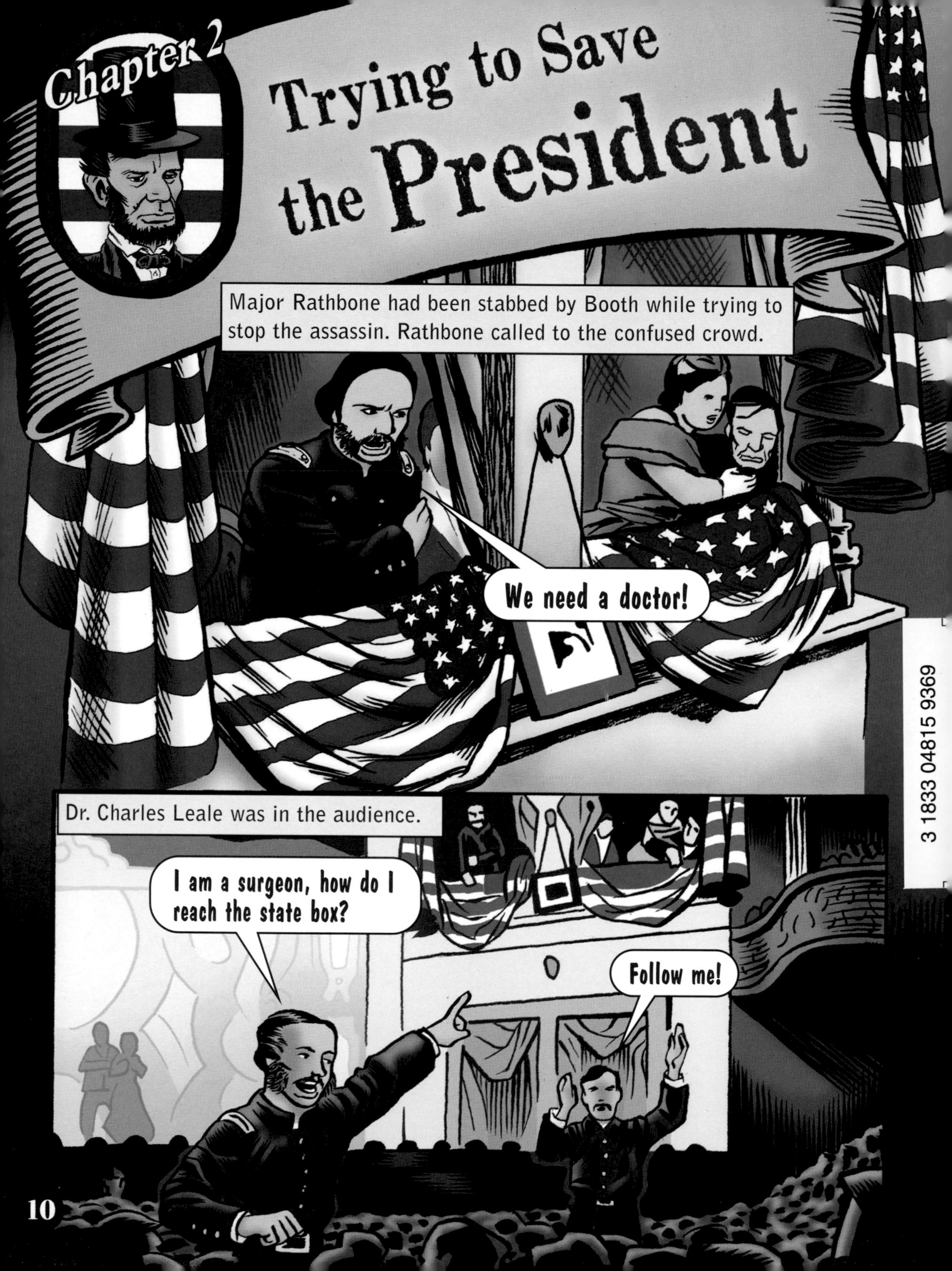
Major Rathbone had been stabbed by Booth while trying to stop the assassin. Rathbone called to the confused crowd.
We need a doctor!
Dr. Charles Leale was in the audience.
I am a surgeon, how do I reach the state box?
Follow me!

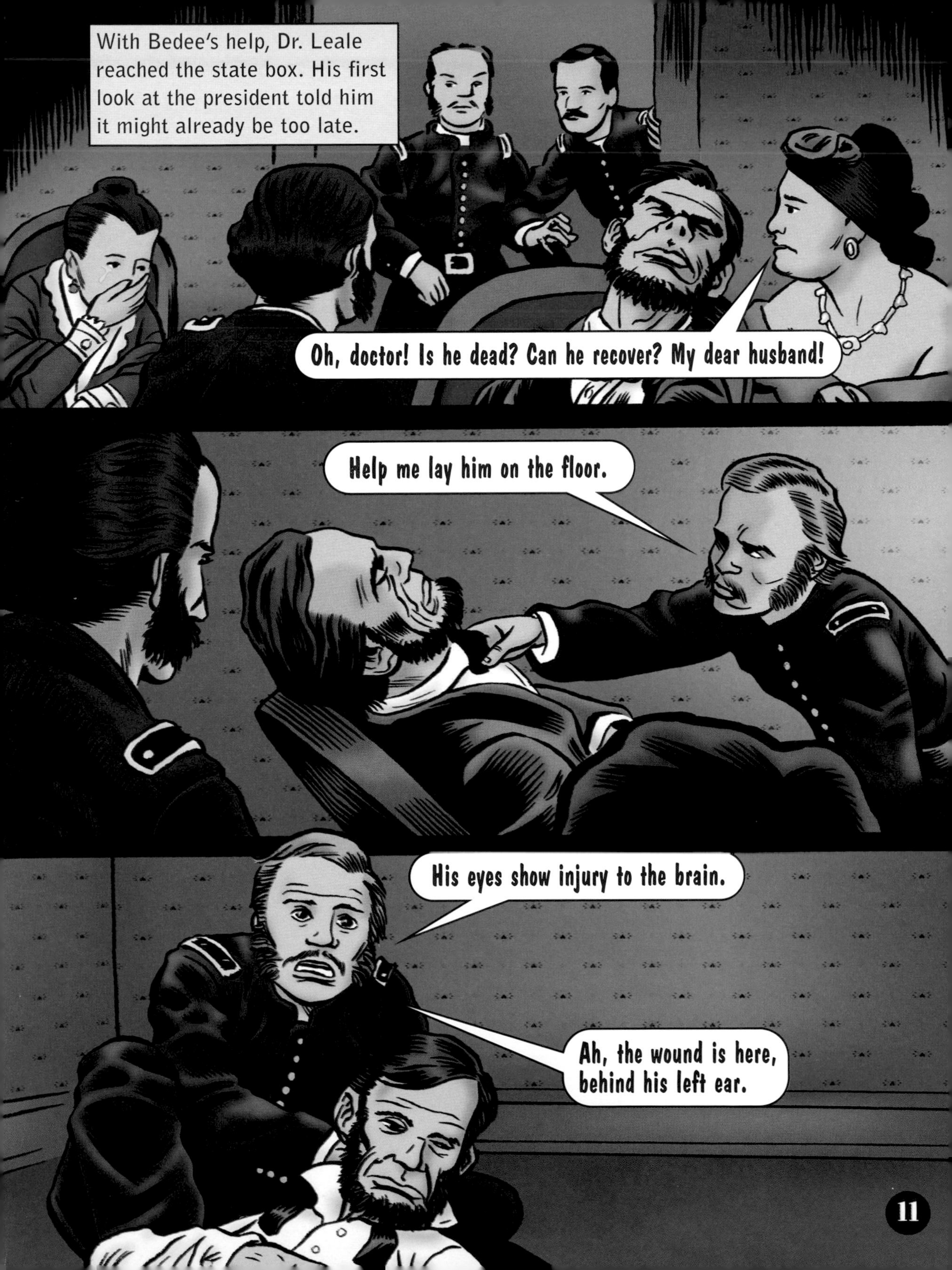
With Bedee's help, Dr. Leale reached the state box. His first look at the president told him it might already be too late.
Oh, doctor! Is he dead? Can he recover? My dear husband!
Help me lay him on the floor.
His eyes show injury to the brain.
Ah, the wound is here, behind his left ear.

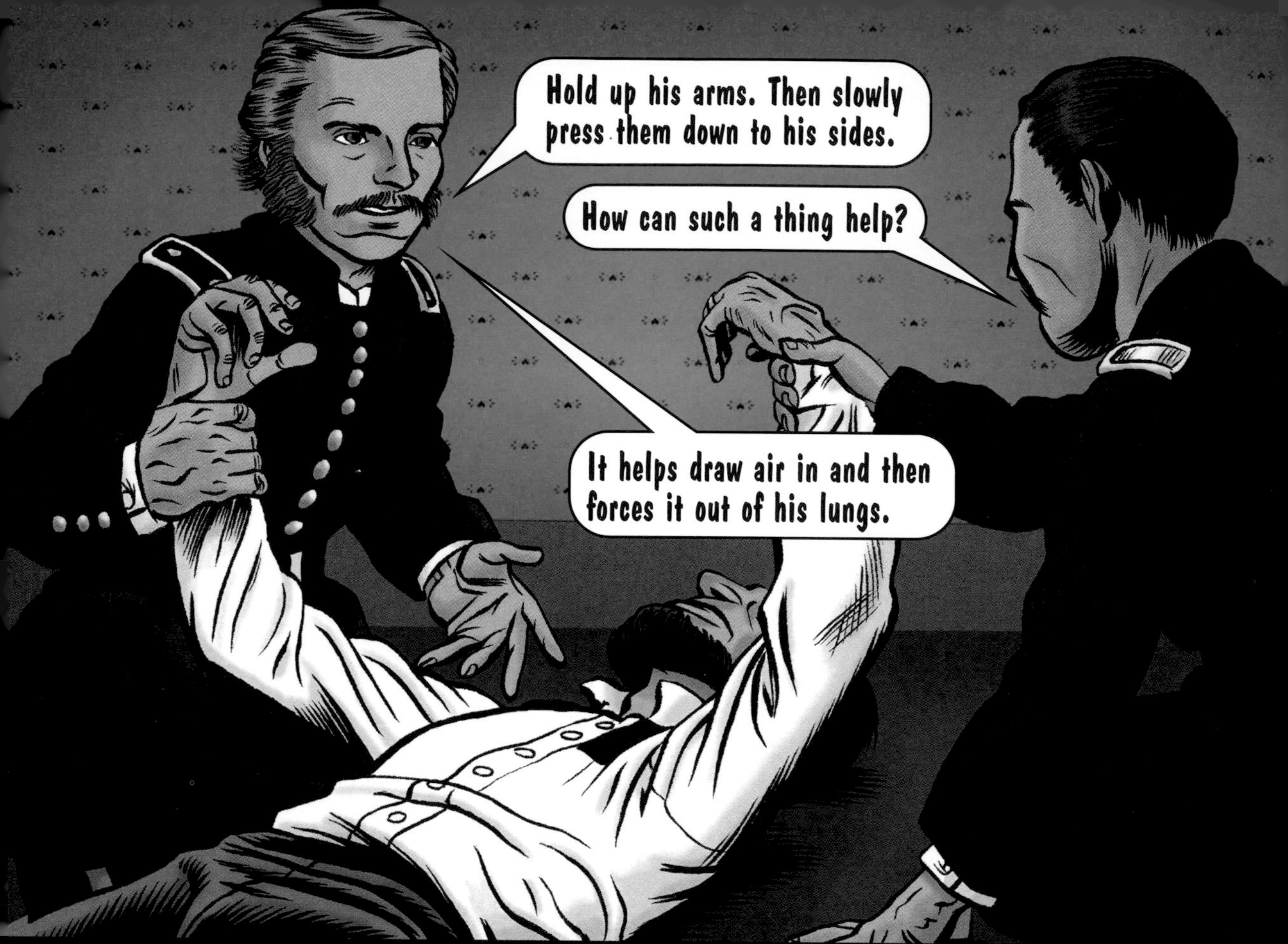
Hold up his arms. Then slowly press them down to his sides.
How can such a thing help?
It helps draw air in and then forces it out of his lungs.

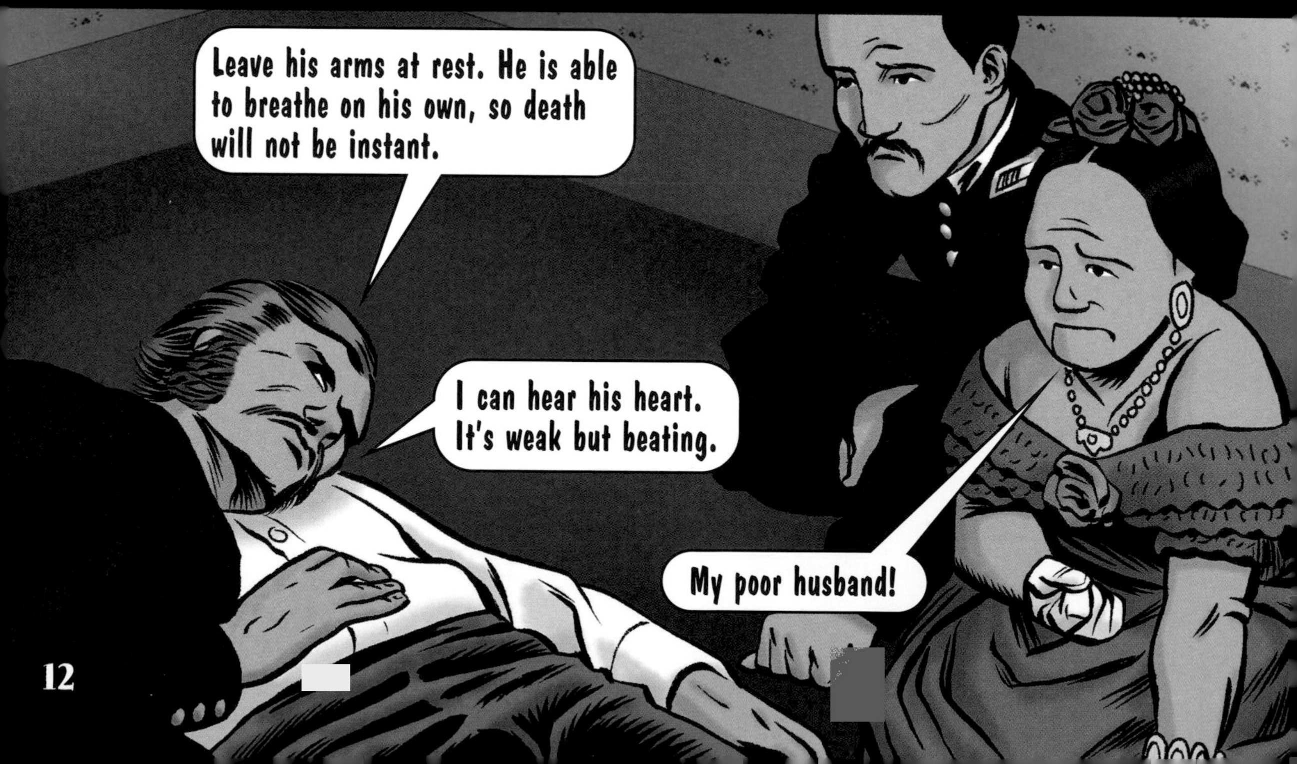
Leave his arms at rest. He is able to breathe on his own, so death will not be instant.
I can hear his heart. It's weak but beating.
My poor husband!

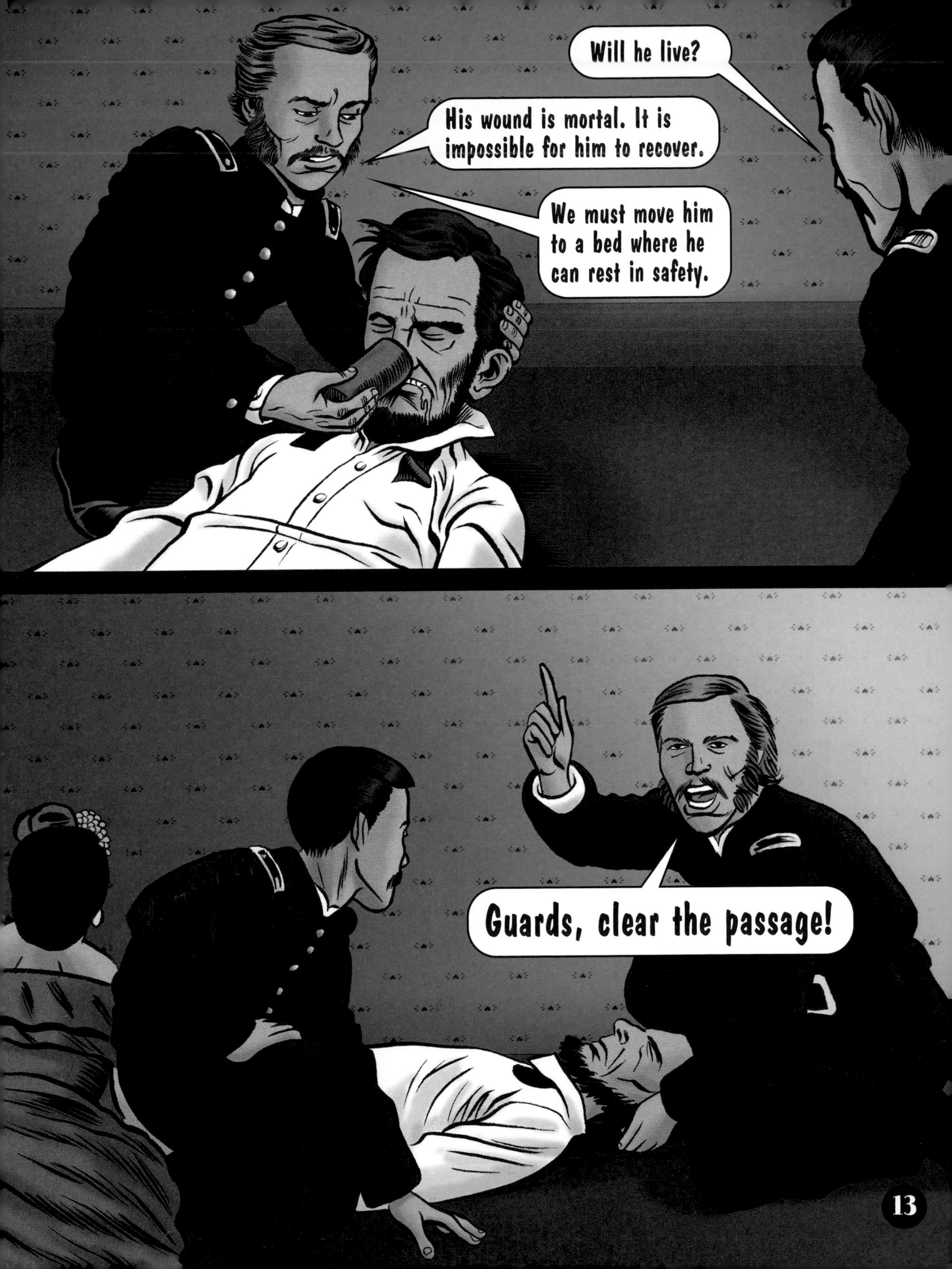
Will he live?
His wound is mortal. It is impossible for him to recover.
We must move him to a bed where he can rest in safety.
Guards, clear the passage!

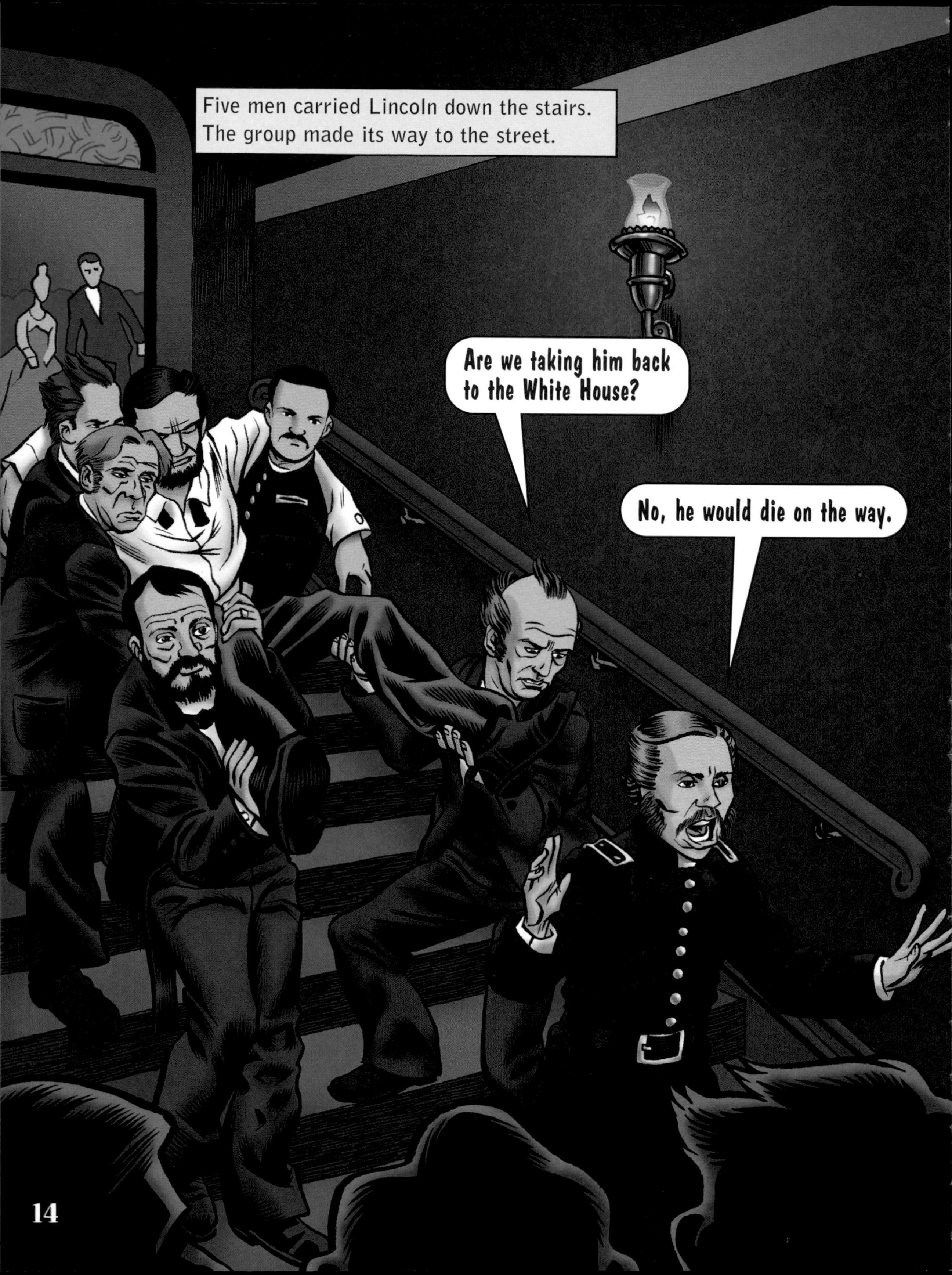
Five men carried Lincoln down the stairs.
The group made its way to the street.
Are we taking him back to the White House?
No, he would die on the way.

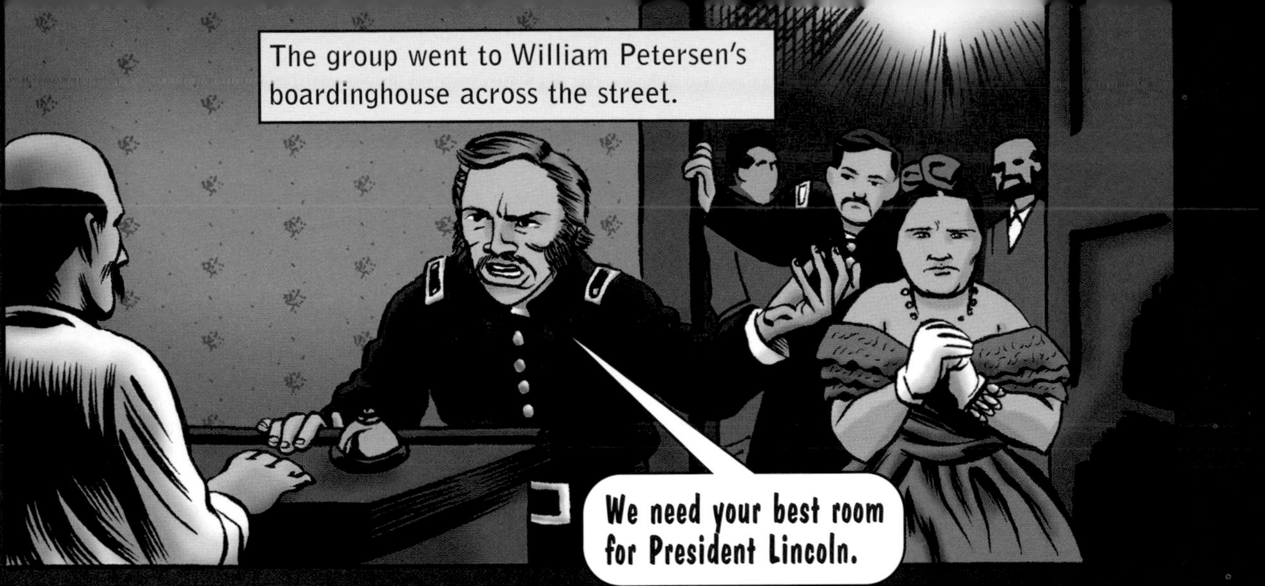
The group went to William Petersen's boardinghouse across the street.
We need your best room for President Lincoln.

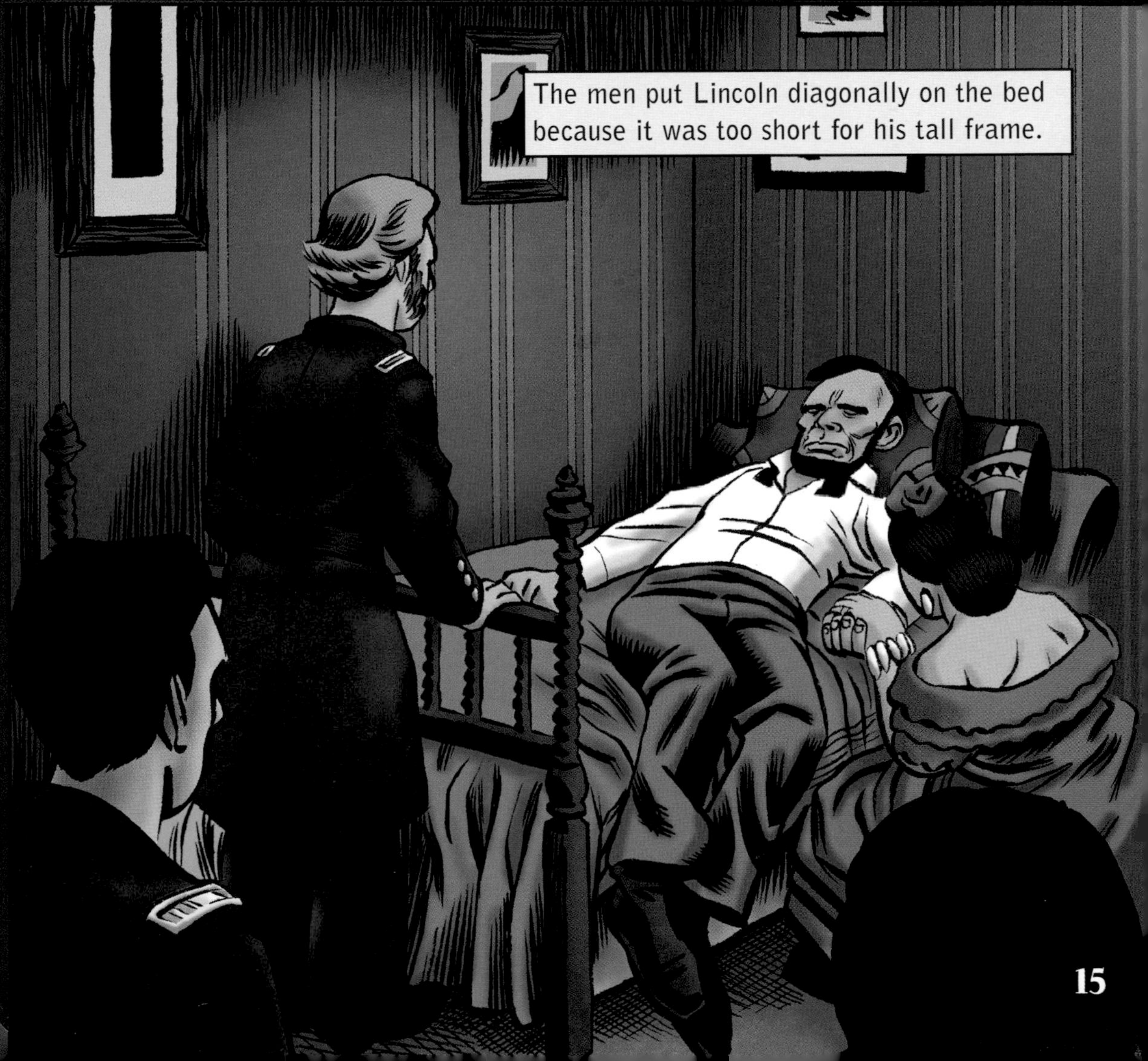
The men put Lincoln diagonally on the bed because it was too short for his tall frame.

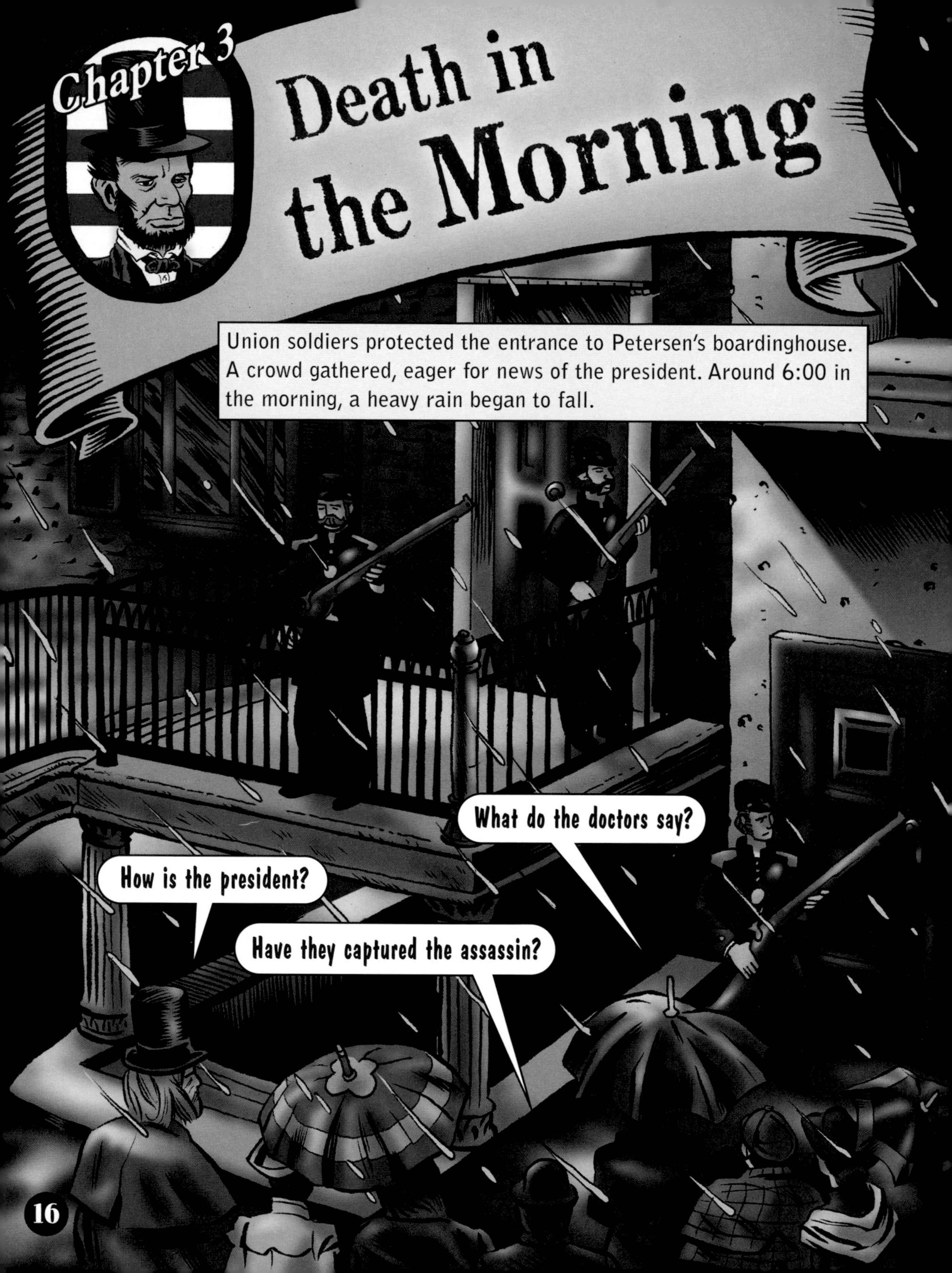
Chapter 3
Death in the Morning
Union soldiers protected the entrance to Petersen's boardinghouse. A crowd gathered, eager for news of the president. Around 6:00 in the morning, a heavy rain began to fall.
How is the president?
What do the doctors say?
Have they captured the assassin?

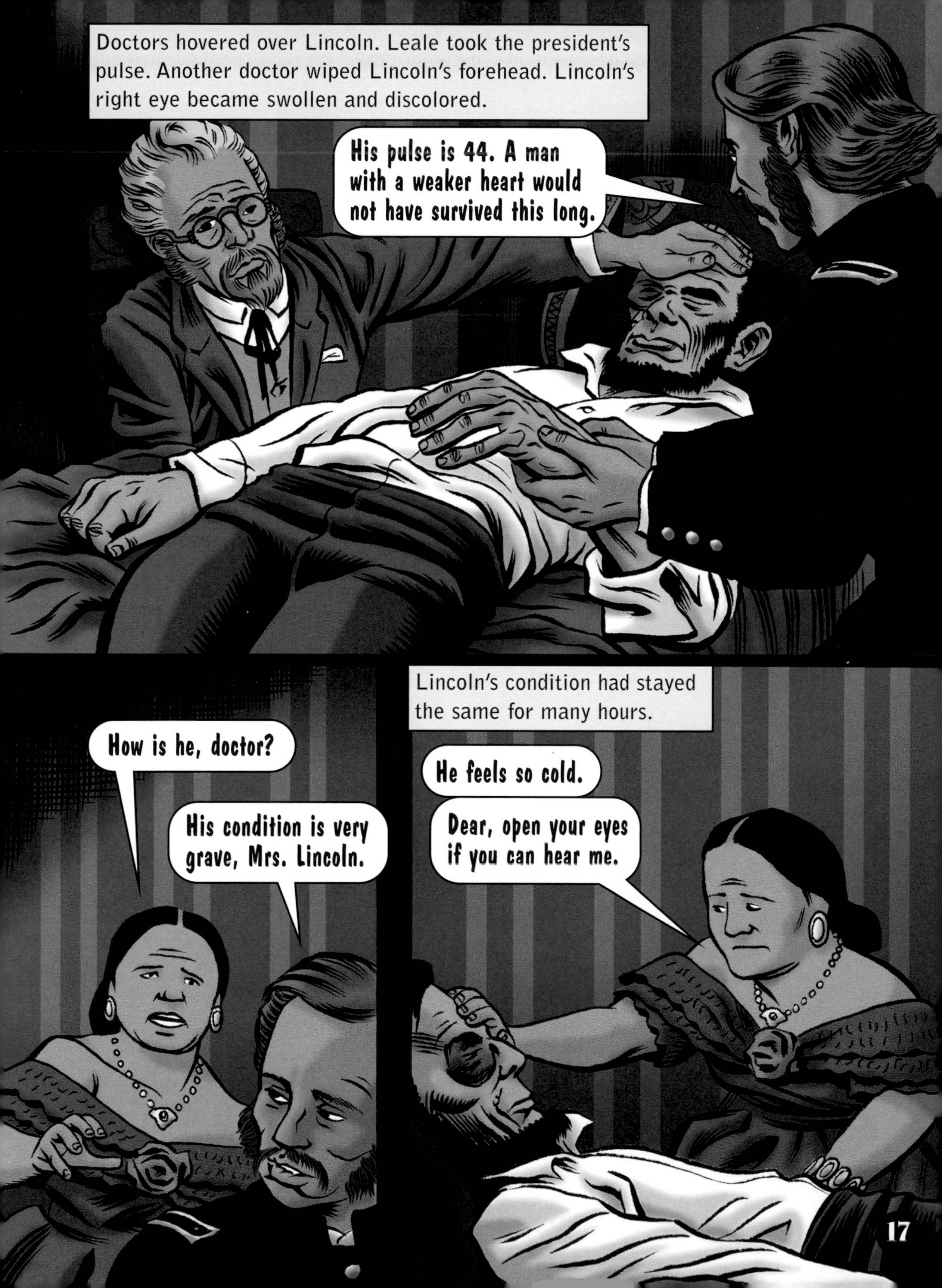
Doctors hovered over Lincoln. Leale took the president's pulse. Another doctor wiped Lincoln's forehead. Lincoln's right eye became swollen and discolored.
His pulse is 44. A man with a weaker heart would not have survived this long.
How is he, doctor?
His condition is very grave, Mrs. Lincoln.
Lincoln's condition had stayed the same for many hours.
He feels so cold.
Dear, open your eyes if you can hear me.

Robert, Lincoln's oldest son, had been at the White House when his father was shot. Upon hearing the news, Robert immediately went to Petersen's boardinghouse. He tried to calm his mother throughout the night.

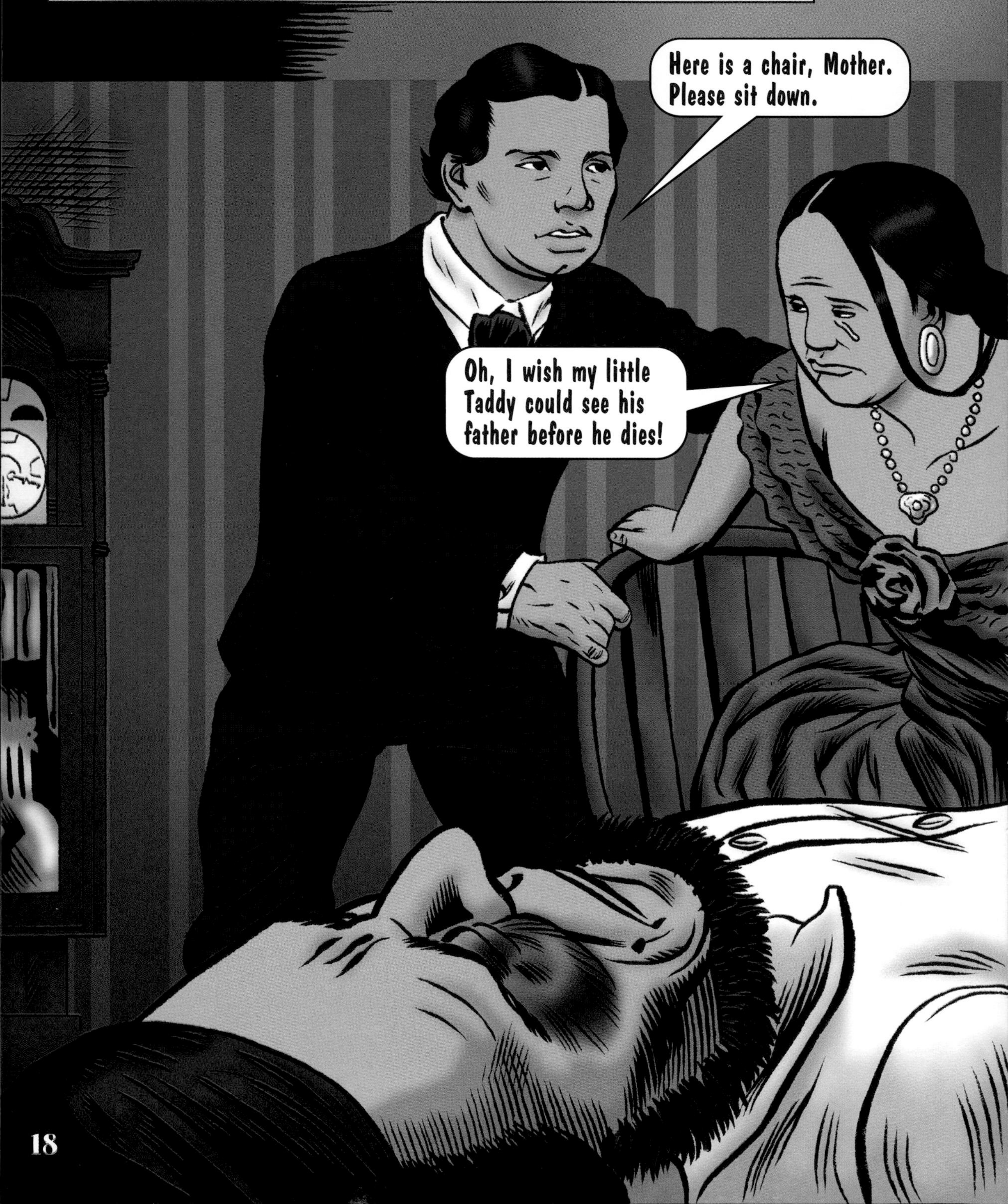
Here is a chair, Mother. Please sit down.
Oh, I wish my little Taddy could see his father before he dies!

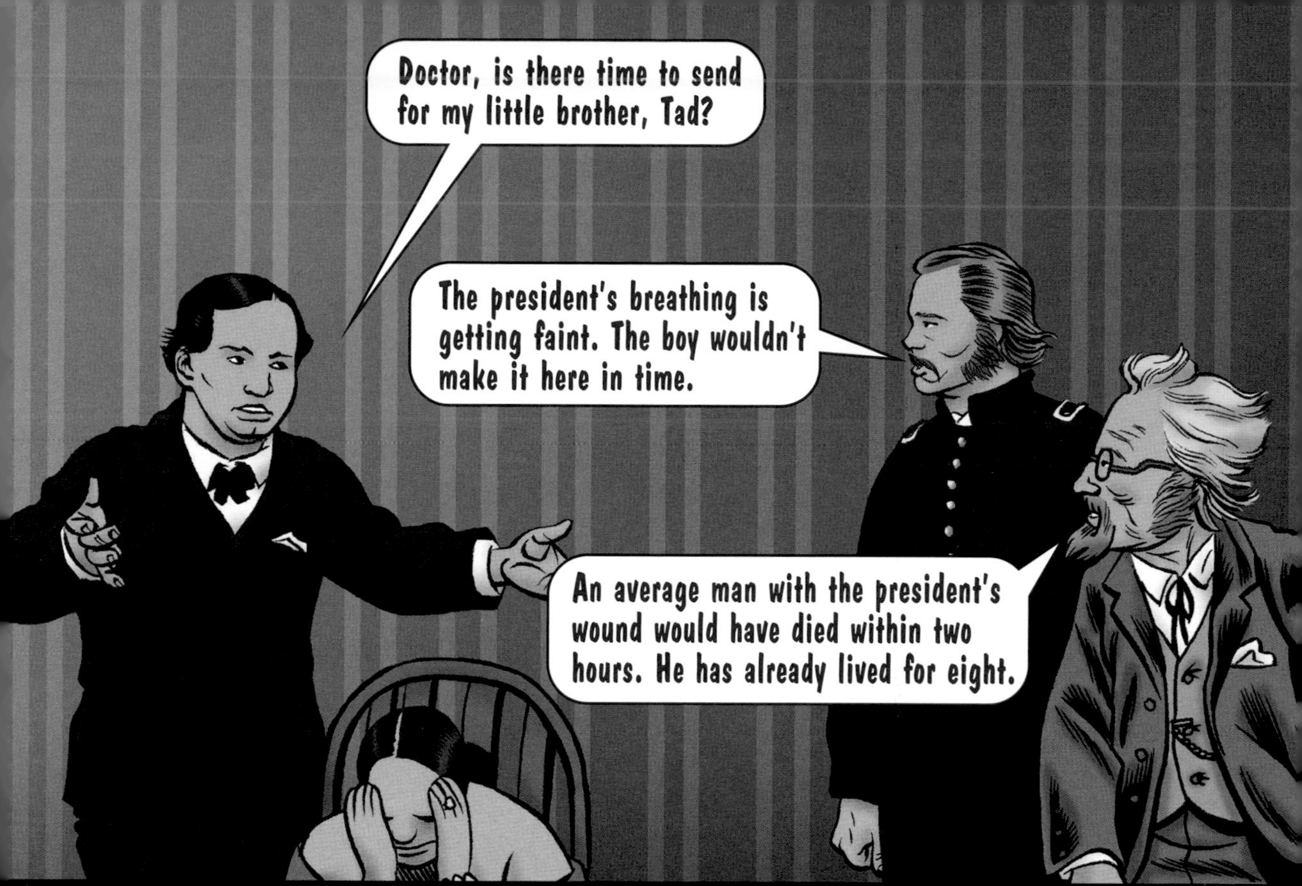
Doctor, is there time to send for my little brother, Tad?
The president's breathing is getting faint. The boy wouldn't make it here in time.
An average man with the president's wound would have died within two hours. He has already lived for eight.

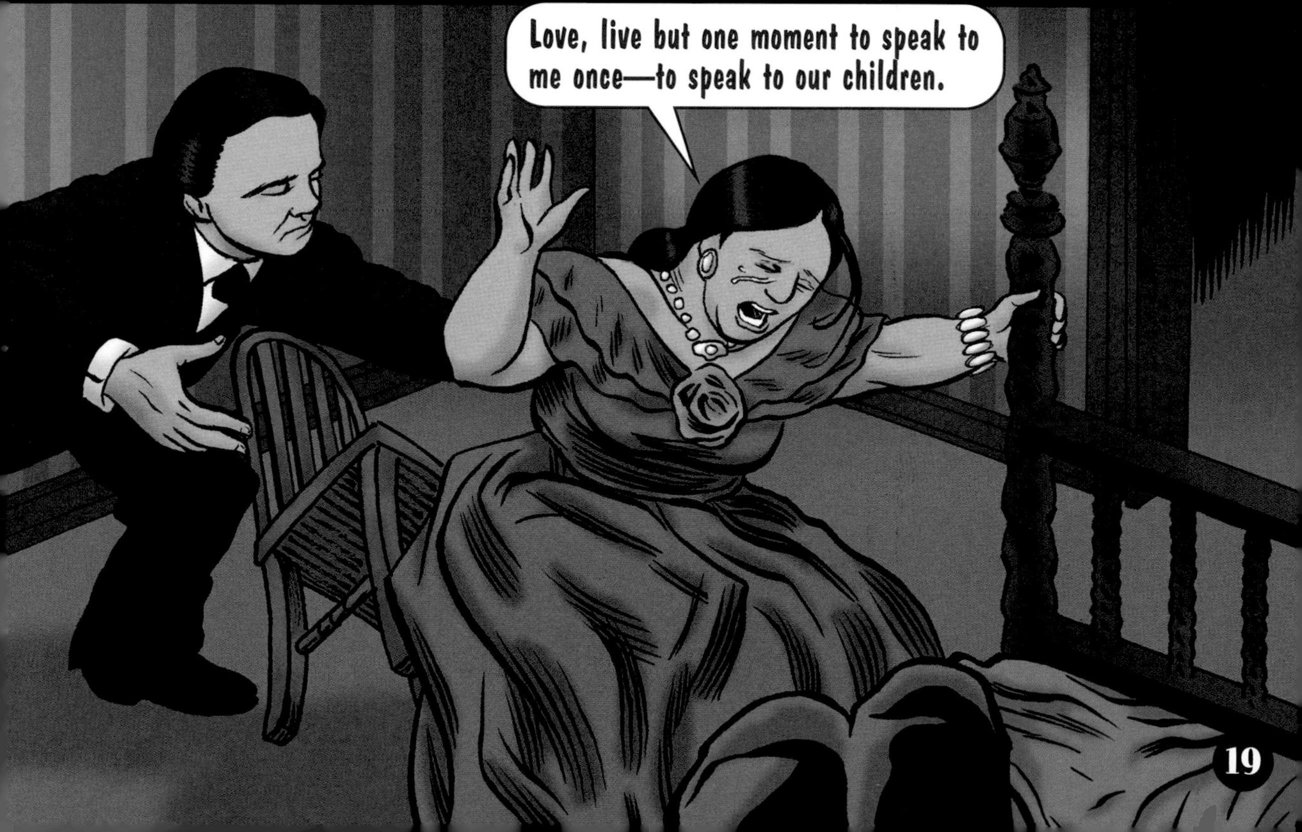
Love, live but one moment to speak to me once—to speak to our children.

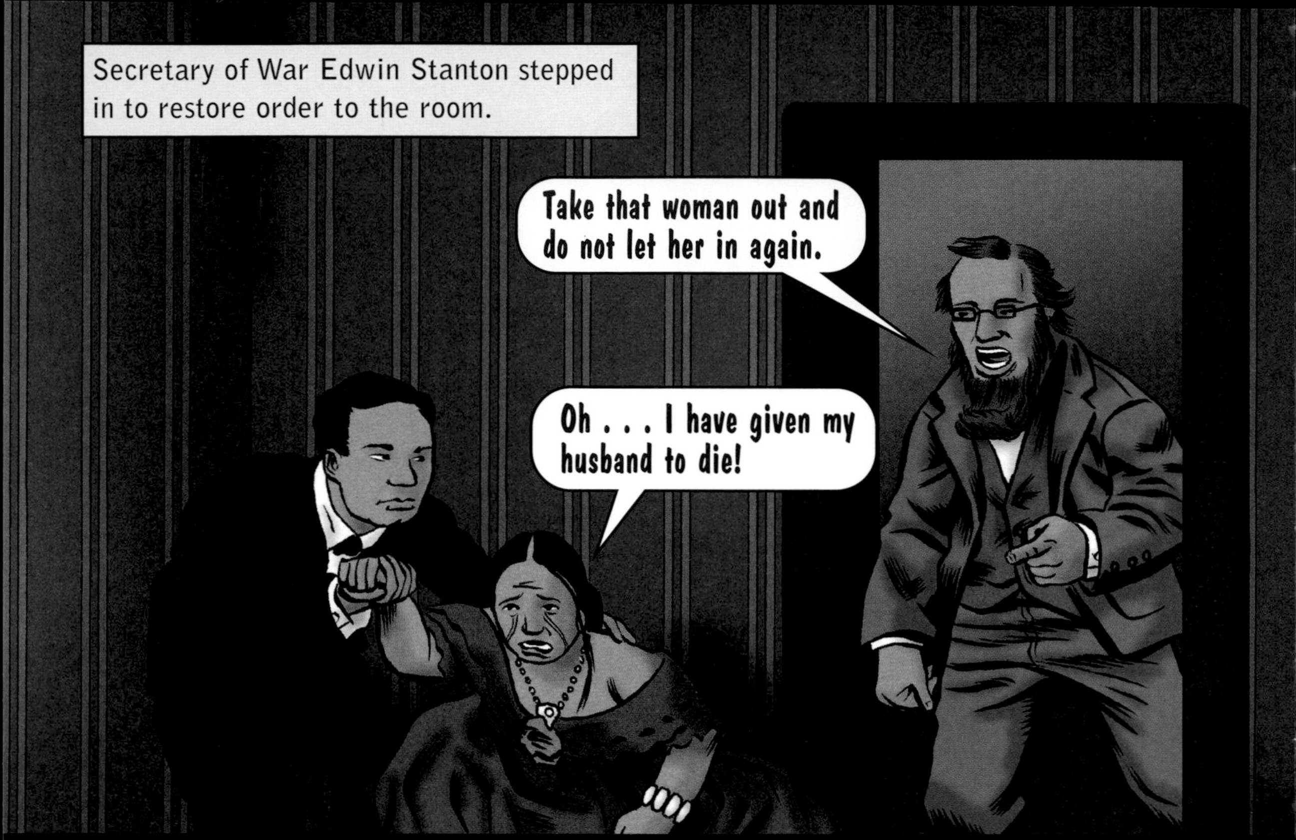
Secretary of War Edwin Stanton stepped in to restore order to the room.
Take that woman out and do not let her in again.
Oh . . . I have given my husband to die!

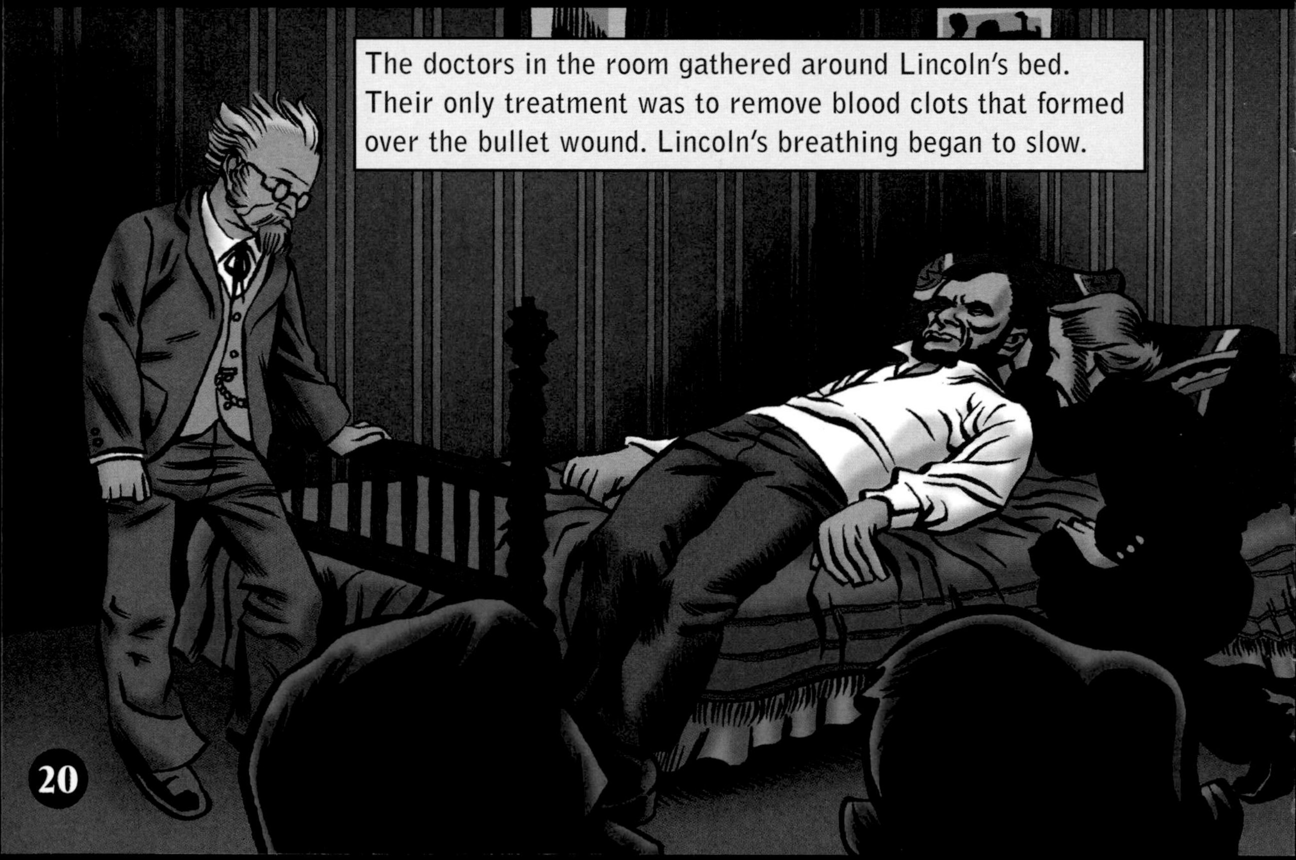
The doctors in the room gathered around Lincoln's bed. Their only treatment was to remove blood clots that formed over the bullet wound. Lincoln's breathing began to slow.

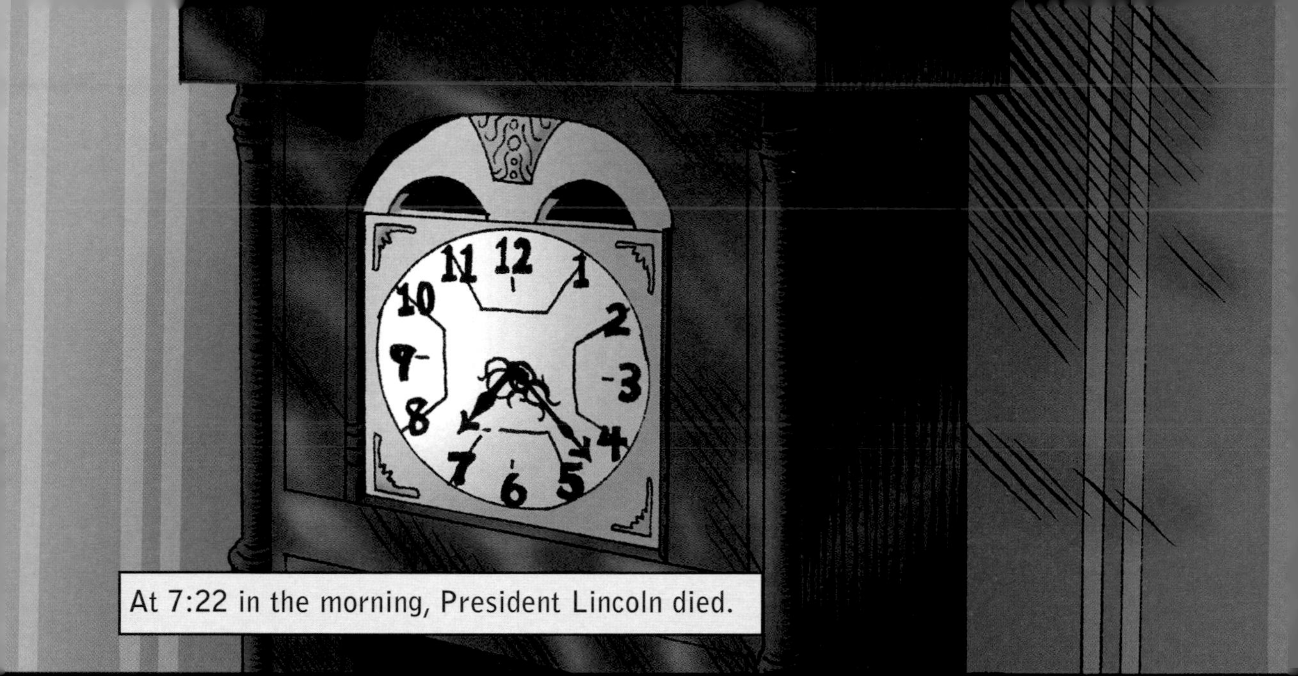
At 7:22 in the morning, President Lincoln died.

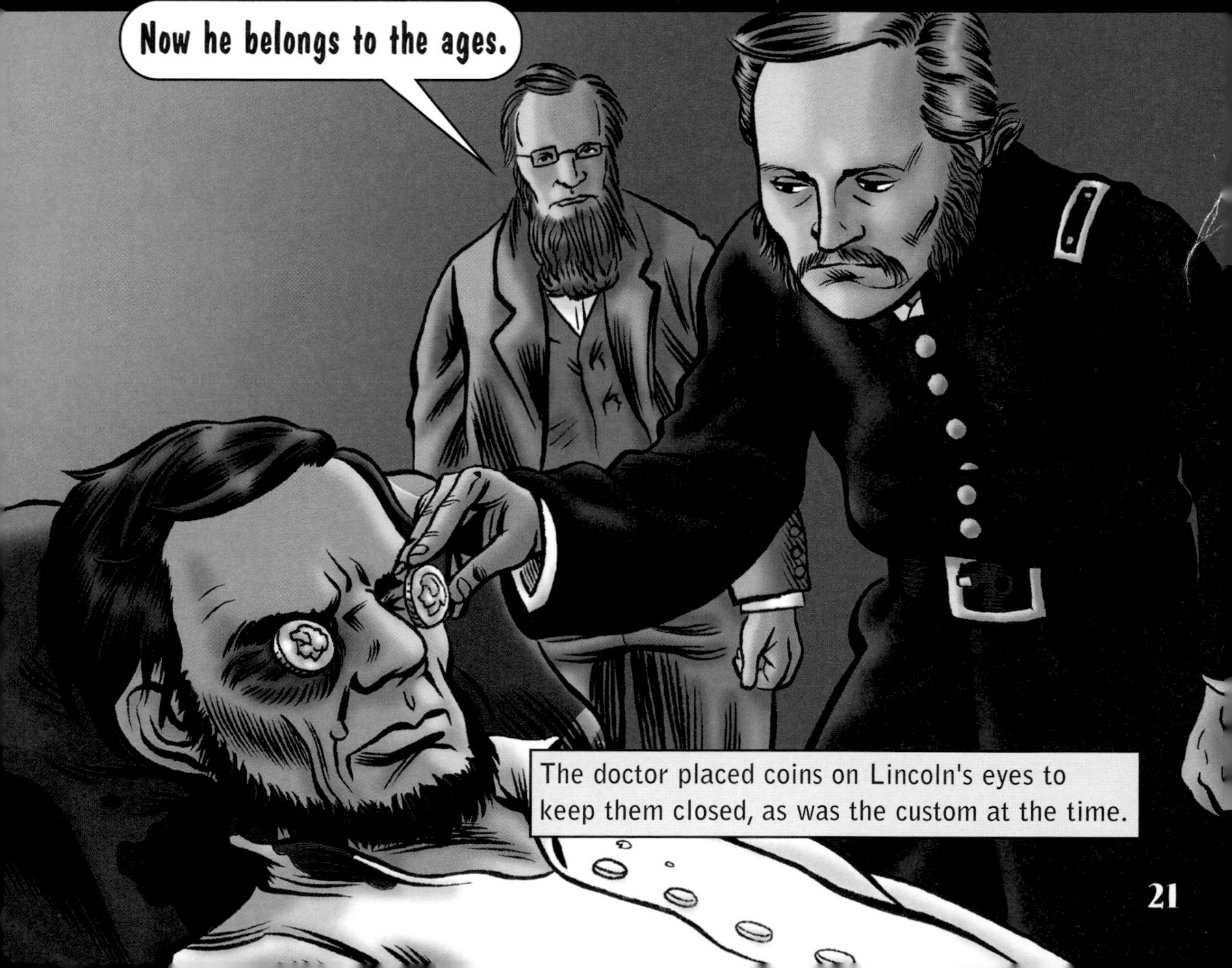
Now he belongs to the ages.
The doctor placed coins on Lincoln's eyes to keep them closed, as was the custom at the time.

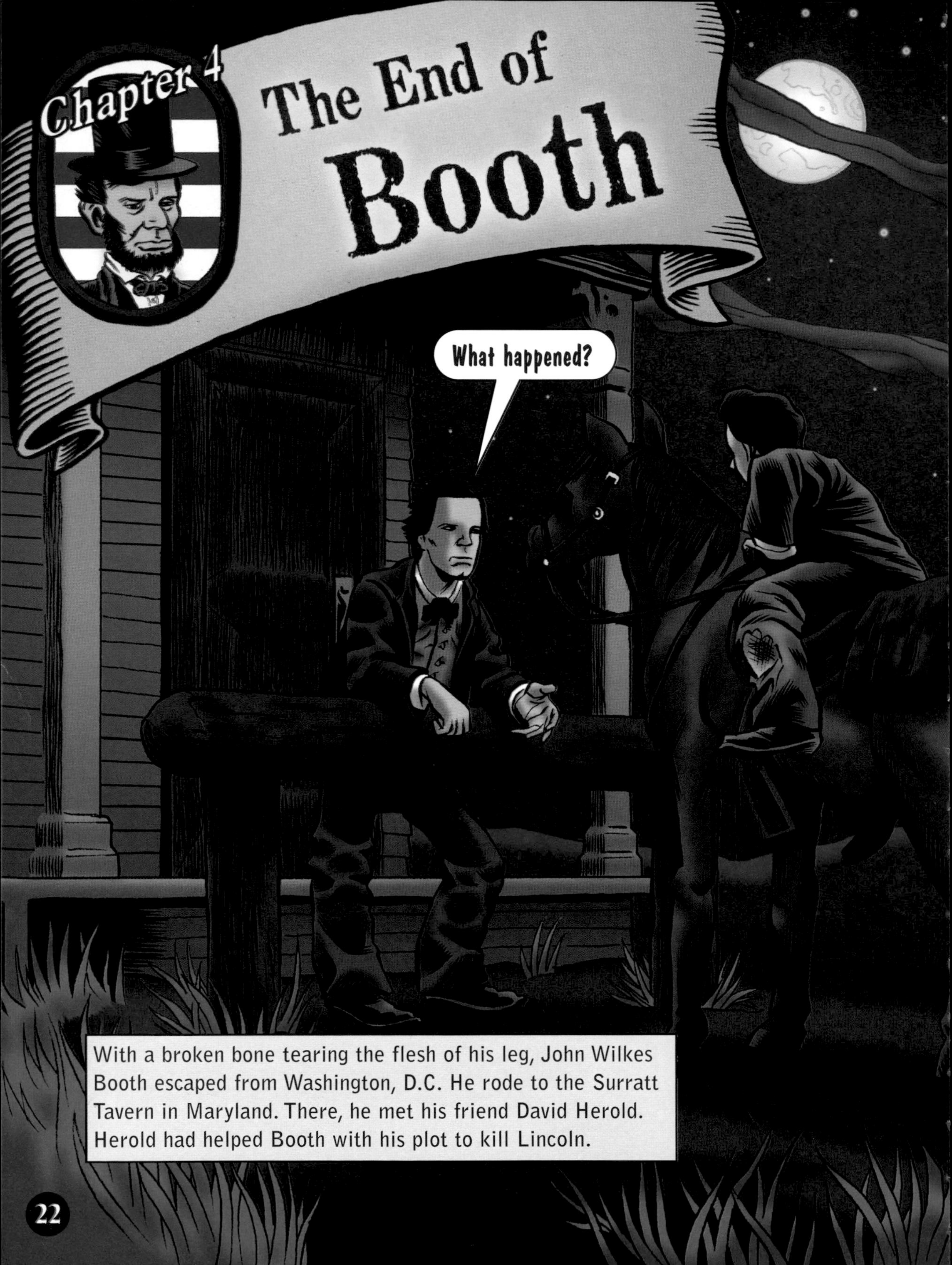
Chapter 4
The End of Booth
What happened?
With a broken bone tearing the flesh of his leg, John Wilkes Booth escaped from Washington, D.C. He rode to the Surratt Tavern in Maryland. There, he met his friend David Herold. Herold had helped Booth with his plot to kill Lincoln.

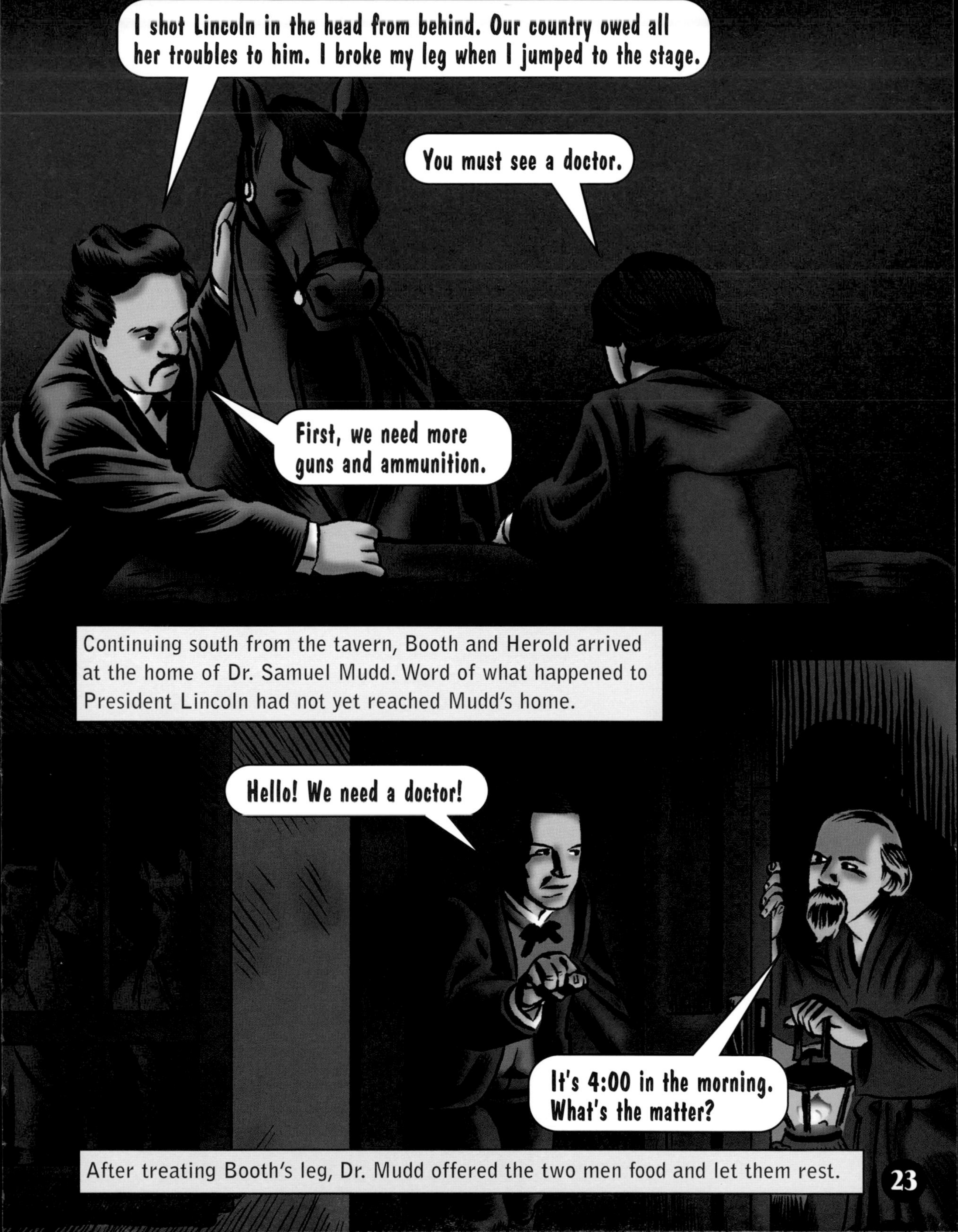
I shot Lincoln in the head from behind. Our country owed all her troubles to him. I broke my leg when I jumped to the stage.
You must see a doctor.
First, we need more guns and ammunition.
Continuing south from the tavern, Booth and Herold arrived at the home of Dr. Samuel Mudd. Word of what happened to President Lincoln had not yet reached Mudd's home.
Hello! We need a doctor!
It's 4:00 in the morning. What's the matter?
After treating Booth's leg, Dr. Mudd offered the two men food and let them rest.

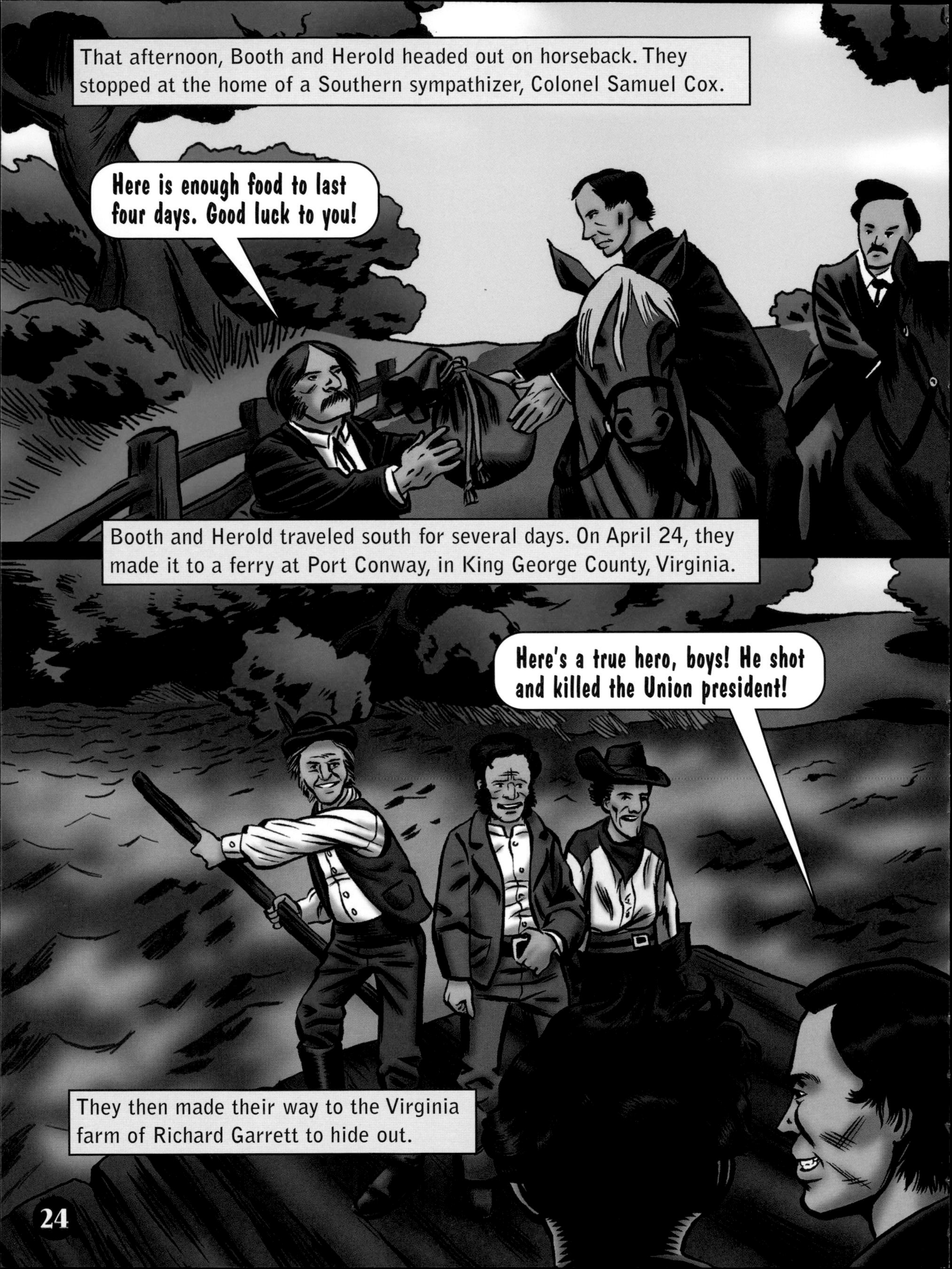
That afternoon, Booth and Herold headed out on horseback. They stopped at the home of a Southern sympathizer, Colonel Samuel Cox.
Here is enough food to last four days. Good luck to you!
Booth and Herold traveled south for several days. On April 24, they made it to a ferry at Port Conway, in King George County, Virginia.
Here's a true hero, boys! He shot and killed the Union president!
They then made their way to the Virginia farm of Richard Garrett to hide out.

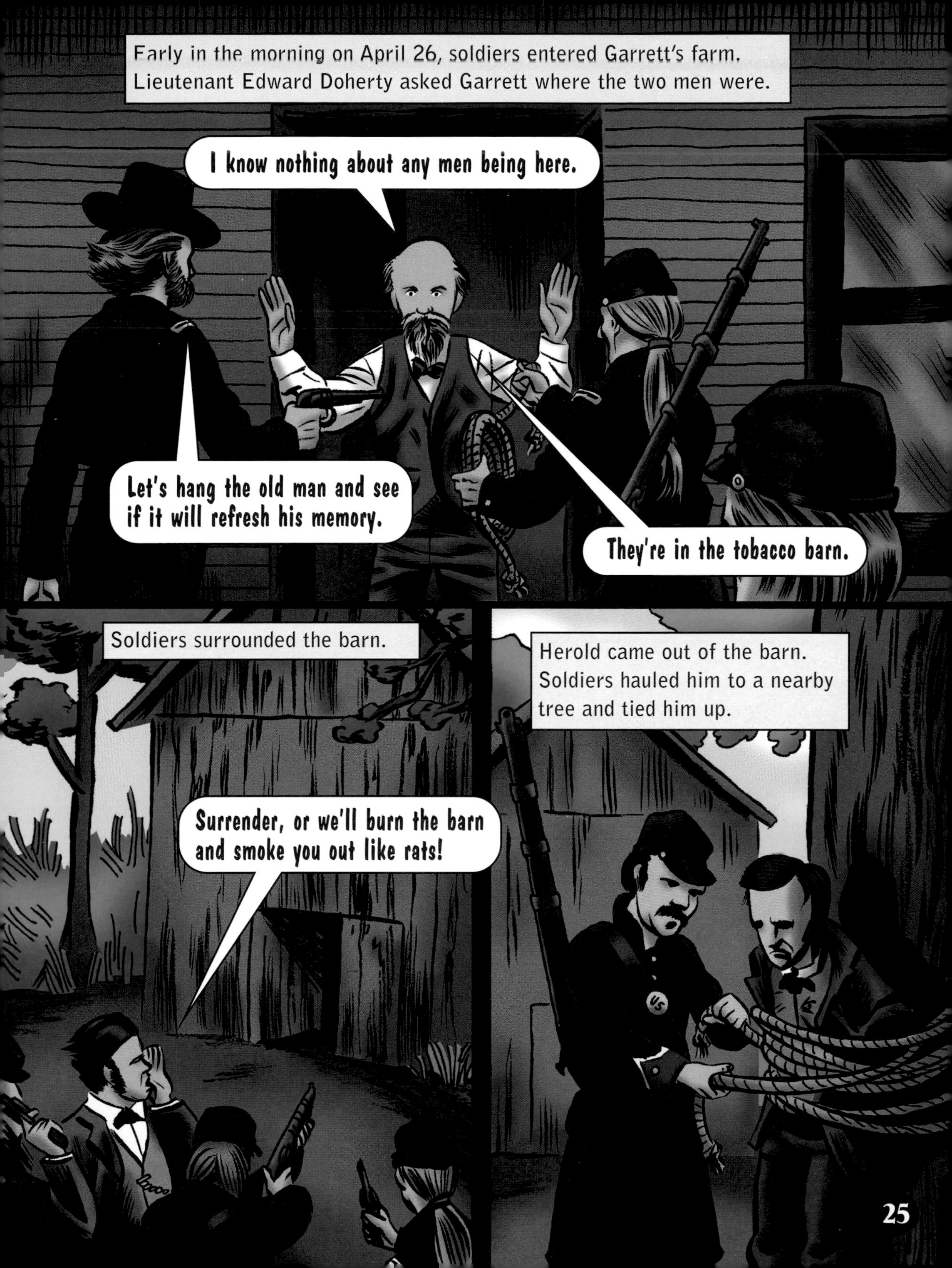
Early in the morning on April 26, soldiers entered Garrett's farm. Lieutenant Edward Doherty asked Garrett where the two men were.
I know nothing about any men being here.
Let's hang the old man and see if it will refresh his memory.
They're in the tobacco barn.
Soldiers surrounded the barn.
Surrender, or we'll burn the barn and smoke you out like rats!
Herold came out of the barn. Soldiers hauled him to a nearby tree and tied him up.

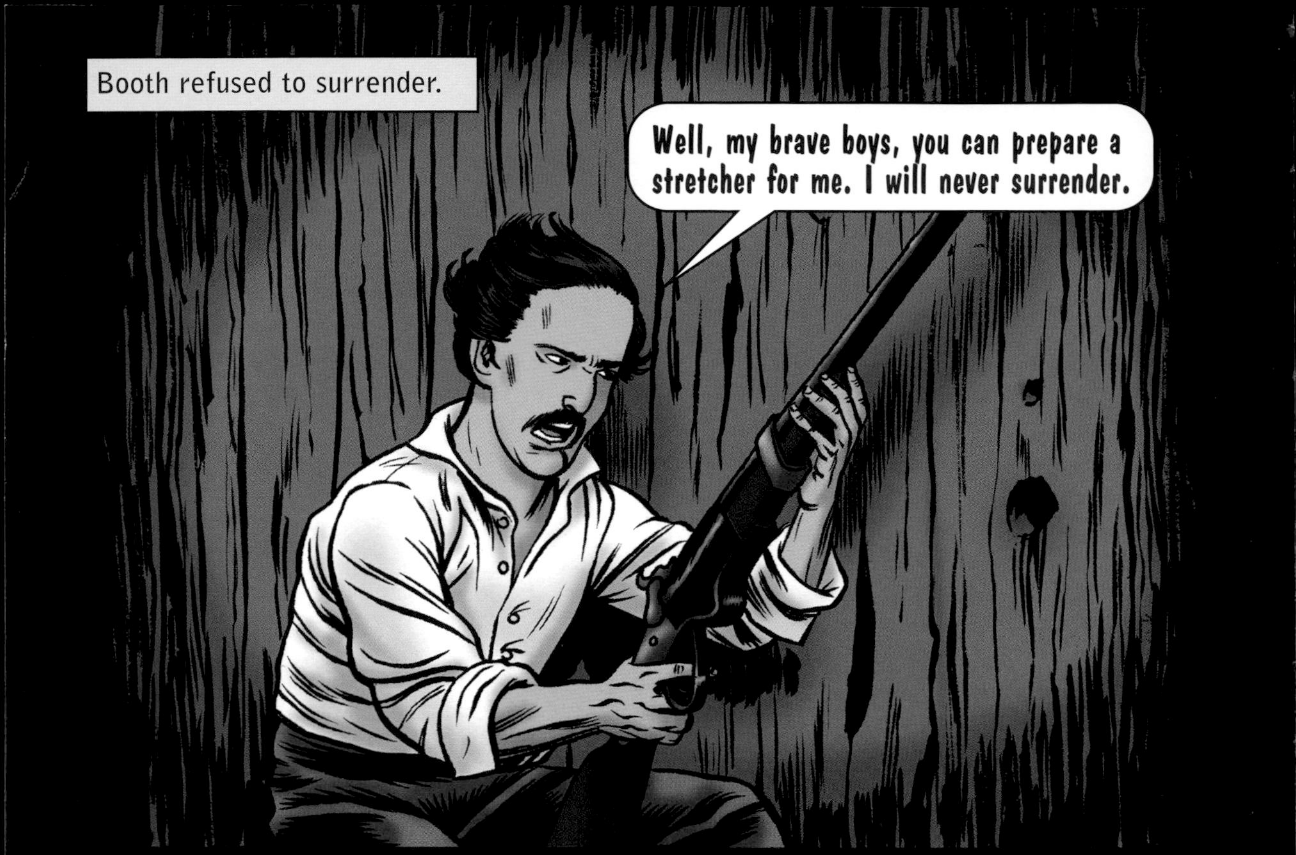
Booth refused to surrender.
Well, my brave boys, you can prepare a stretcher for me. I will never surrender.

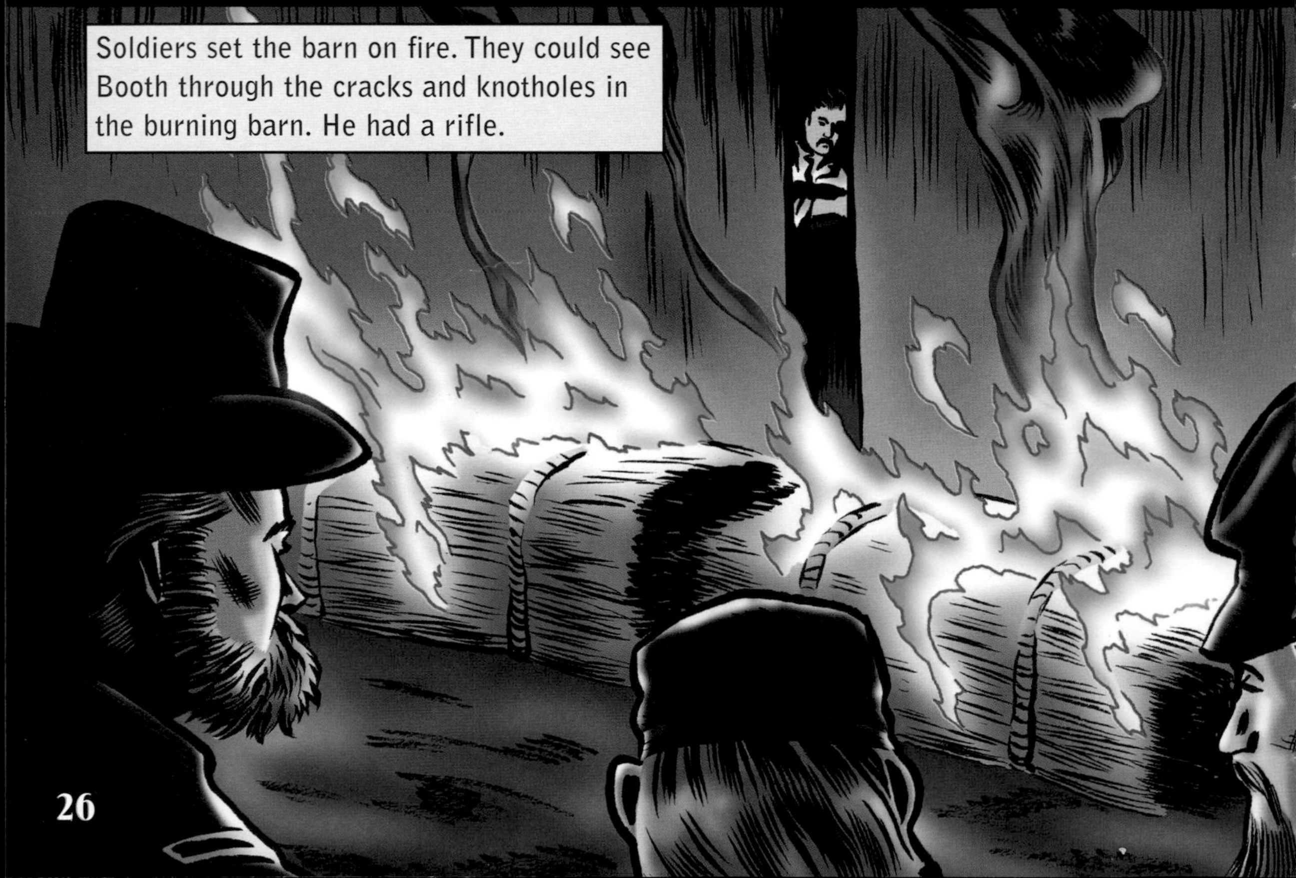
Soldiers set the barn on fire. They could see Booth through the cracks and knotholes in the burning barn. He had a rifle.

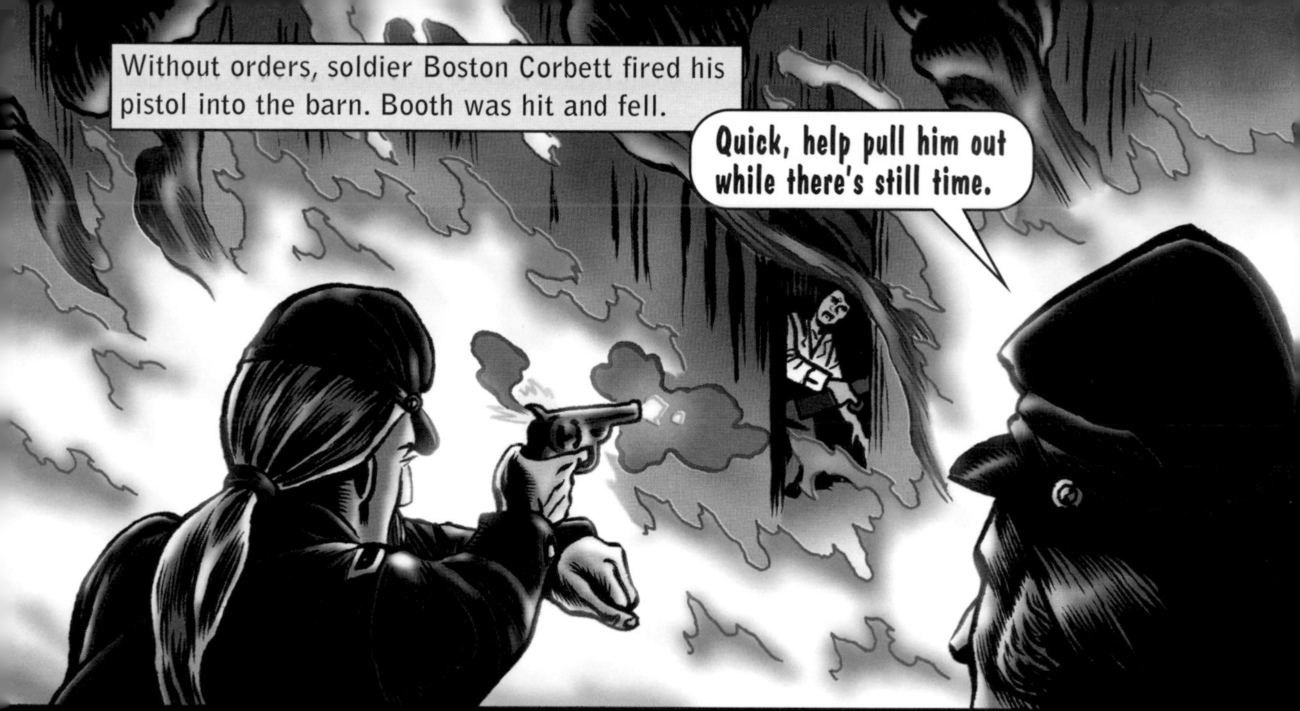
Without orders, soldier Boston Corbett fired his pistol into the barn. Booth was hit and fell.
Quick, help pull him out while there's still time.

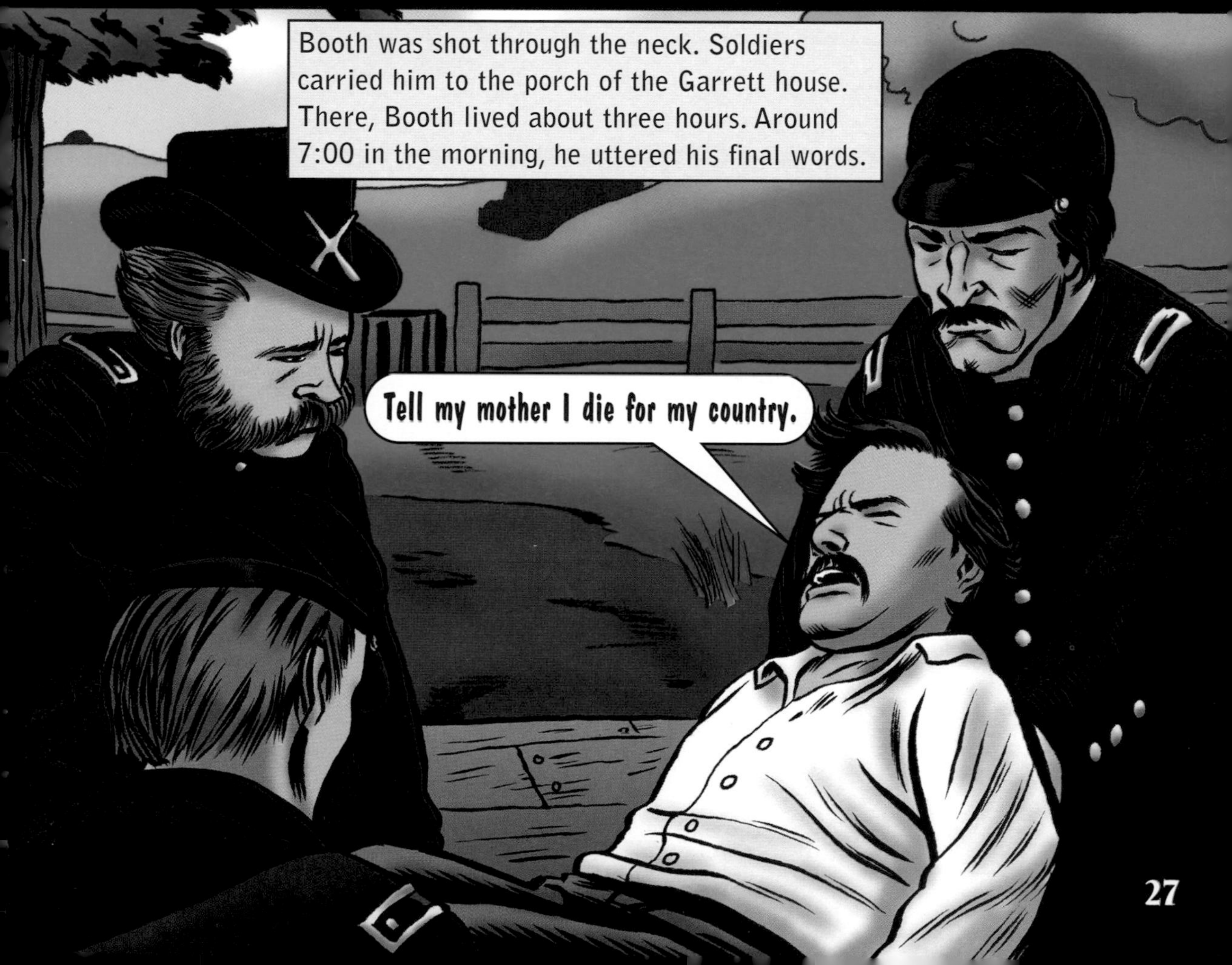
Booth was shot through the neck. Soldiers carried him to the porch of the Garrett house. There, Booth lived about three hours. Around 7:00 in the morning, he uttered his final words.
Tell my mother I die for my country.

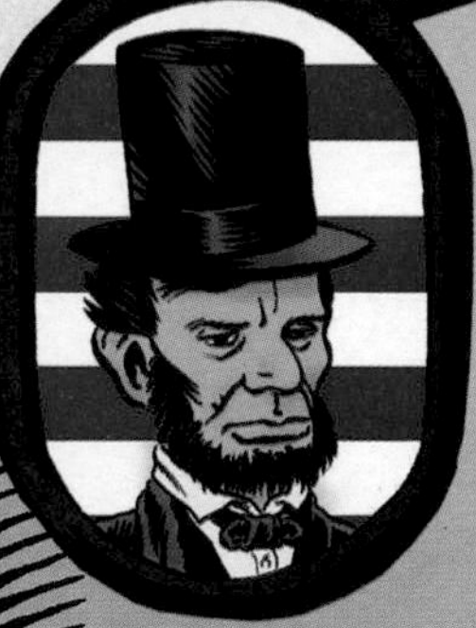

More about Lincoln and the Assassination

- The Civil War began on April 12, 1861. Confederate General Lee surrendered to Union General Grant on April 9, 1865, at Appomattox Court House in Virginia. Five days later, Lincoln was assassinated.

- In March 1865, John Wilkes Booth visited Charles Warwick, a friend and fellow actor. Warwick was living in a room at the Petersen boardinghouse. During his visit, Warwick let Booth take a nap on the bed. One month later, President Lincoln died on the same bed.

- Booth's deed was part of a conspiracy. Confederate sympathizers wanted to create chaos in the federal government. They planned to kill the president, vice president, secretary of state, and Union General Grant. Lincoln was the only one to actually die.

- The U.S. government charged eight people with the conspiracy. Four people were sentenced to be hanged, three to life in prison, and one to a six-year prison term.

- Abraham Lincoln was born February 12, 1809. When he died on April 15, 1865, he was 56 years old.

Lincoln was inaugurated as the 16th president on March 4, 1861. He was reelected to a second term, which began on March 4, 1865.

 Lincoln was the first president to be photographed at his inauguration. John Wilkes Booth can be seen standing close to Lincoln in the picture.

 Lincoln was the first president to have a beard while in office.

 At 6 feet, 4 inches tall, Lincoln was the tallest president.

 Vice President Andrew Johnson became president on April 15, 1865, hours after Lincoln died.

Each fall and spring, the Surratt Society sponsors bus tours along Booth's escape route. People can also follow Booth's path by car. Today, the route has paved roads and is lined with businesses. In 1865, it was a muddy, swampy path.

Glossary

assassin (uh-SASS-uhn)—a person who murders a well-known or important person, such as a president

chaos (KAY-oss)—total confusion

conspiracy (kuhn-SPIHR-uh-see)—a secret, illegal plan made by two or more people

ferry (FER-ee)—a boat or ship that regularly carries people across a stretch of water

mortal (MOR-tuhl)—causing death; Lincoln's gunshot wound was mortal.

plot (PLOT)—to plan in secret, usually to do something wrong or illegal

sympathizer (SIM-puh-thyz-uhr)—a person who supports a group or a cause

tyrant (TYE-ruhnt)—someone who rules other people in a cruel or unjust way

Internet Sites

FactHound offers a safe, fun way to find Internet sites related to this book. All of the sites on FactHound have been researched by our staff.

Here's how:

1. Visit *www.facthound.com*
2. Type in this special code **0736838317** for age-appropriate sites. Or enter a search word related to this book for a more general search.
3. Click on the **Fetch It** button.

FactHound will fetch the best sites for you!

Read More

Burgan, Michael. *The Assassination of Abraham Lincoln*. We the People. Minneapolis: Compass Point Books, 2004.

Marinelli, Deborah A. *The Assassination of Abraham Lincoln*. The Library of Political Assassinations. New York: Rosen, 2002.

Oberle, Lora Polack. *Abraham Lincoln*. Let Freedom Ring. Mankato, Minn.: Bridgestone Books, 2002.

Schott, Jane A. *Abraham Lincoln*. History Maker Bios. Minneapolis: Lerner, 2002.

Zeinert, Karen. *The Lincoln Murder Plot*. North Haven, Conn.: Linnet Books, 1999.

Bibliography

Bishop, Jim. *The Day Lincoln Was Shot*. New York: Harper & Row, 1955.

Bryan, George S. *The Great American Myth*. Chicago: Americana House, 1990.

Ford's Theatre National Historic Site. http://www.nps.gov/foth/index2.htm.

Kunhardt, Dorothy Meserve, and Philip B. Kunhardt Jr. *Twenty Days*. New York: Castle Books, 1965.

Norton, Roger. Abraham Lincoln Research Site. http://members.aol.com/RVSNorton/Lincoln2.html.

Steers, Edward Jr. *Blood on the Moon: The Assassination of Abraham Lincoln*. Lexington: University Press of Kentucky, 2001.

Index